RANT OF A RETAILER

Macy May Marcus

Table of Contents

<u>Dedication</u>

To my mother, Susan, who gave me everything I needed to start this book.

And to my husband, Charlie, who gave me everything I needed to finish it.

And to all the customers out there who hang up clothes after trying them on.

You know who you are.

Introduction

On my very first day as a manager at a major department store, I wore a pencil skirt, a blazer, and four-inch black heels.

Five hours into my shift, I was on the floor on my knees, grinding my Calvin Klein skirt into the tile, folding approximately 3,000 printed t-shirts, feet blistered in my Charles David heels, and I asked myself, *"How did I get here?"*

Let's back up. After graduating from a top 25 business school with a MBA when I was twenty-six years old, I was a rock star in my own mind. I had an MBA! I was brilliant! I deserved to make $150,000 a year, minimum! Bring on the company car, the petty cash fund, and the corner office!

Nine months of job searching later, I discovered education doesn't do much for a career without the matching experience.

I applied to be a vice-president of marketing.

Then a marketing manager.

Then an associate marketing manager.

Then a marketing administrative assistant.

Then a janitor. (Hopefully cleaning the floors in the marketing department.)

I had nothing. Nada. No prospects, and absolutely no money. So I crashed a local university's career fair, where I came across a major department store, recruiting for assistant store managers for their training program.

Why not? I liked buying stuff. How hard could retail really be?

Famous last words.

Roughly one of every ten Americans is employed in the retail sector. This means thirty million people will relate to my adventures.

This also means that nine out of ten of you do not fully understand the heartbreak of a destroyed fitting room. The fury over re-folding pants behind a man who is determined to try on every size in stock. The heart-breaking sorrow when you watch a customer let her twins jump on your display bed. In shoes.

I have been in retail for years, long enough to be exposed to all the craziness that goes on in a store. This is my book.

No returns accepted.

Chapter 1

Crazy Customers Make It All Worthwhile

"Two things are infinite: the universe and human stupidity; and I'm not sure about the universe."
-Albert Einstein

The most entertaining parts of my job, bar none, are the crazy customers. It's not a successful day without a crazy customer story. And let me tell you, crazy comes in all shapes and sizes. Crazy knows no race, gender, socioeconomic status, or age. Crazy is the great social equalizer!

Every industry that specializes in customer service has its share of crazy, but retail gets a special kind. Anyone can wander in off the streets into any store and demand customer service. We get the crotchety old ladies, the belligerent middle-aged men, the thieving teenagers, and the incompetent, illiterate, and obstinate any-agers who flood our store on a daily basis. There is no barrier to entry for a store.

These are true customer conversations heard on my sales floor:

Employee: Is there anything else I can do for you?
Customer: You could marry me.
Employee: *Laughs embarrassedly*
Customer: I'm not kidding...really.
Employee: Time for my break!

Customer: I'll buy this teddy bear with this coupon.
Employee: I'm sorry, ma'am. Those bears are for charity so the coupon doesn't work on them.
Customer: But I have a five dollar coupon and the bear is five bucks. I want it.
Employee: Well, all that money goes directly to children with cancer.
Customer: So?

Customer: Excuse me.

Employee: Yes?

Customer: Do you know if this blends? *Holds up blender*

Employee: Hi, how are you today?

Customer: No, thank you.

Customer: *Picks up a shirt, looks at it, and tosses it back on top of a rack*

Employee: *Looks at her*

Customer: What? Pick it up. That's what you're paid for, isn't it?

Customer: *Reads out loud* Jewelry counter. *To her friend* Oh! I bet that's where they have the jewelry!

Customer: Where do I do returns?

Employee: In the far right corner of the store.

Customer: OK. *Walks to the register in front of her, where returns can't be done*

Employee: Um, did you have a return then?

Customer: Yes.

Employee: Customer service is in the far right of the store.

Customer: But I don't have time to walk over there!

Employee: Did you want to open our in-store credit card?

Customer: No! Can you just shut up and scan my items?

Customer: I have a complaint about your customer service girl.

Employee: Oh, I'm sorry, ma'am. What happened?

Customer: She was just too... blah.

Employee: Um, okay. Was she rude?

Customer: No.

Employee: Was she slow?

Customer: No.

Employee: Did she take care of what you needed?

Customer: Yes.

Employee: *Quiet*

Customer: She was just totally blah, like no personality. You should talk to her about that!

Customer: I want to complain about that associate. She was terrible to me over the holidays!

Manager: She wasn't here during the holidays.

Customer: Oh. Well, then, right before.

Customer: Don't you touch my ID!

Employee: What?

Customer: You have a cold! Don't touch that! I don't want your nasty cold!

Employee: It's allergies, ma'am.

Customer: Nice try. Give me that! *Snatches back her ID and walks out*

Customer: I clicked on your website to get my credit card data, and it won't come up!

Employee: Did you check the box to the left, or the box to the right? They look a lot alike. One is for the regular site and one is for the credit card site.

Customer: The box to the right, of *course*.

Employee: I don't mean to question you, ma'am, but are you completely sure you clicked the box to the right?

Customer: Absolutely! I'll even double check...ummm.... no, that can't be right.

Employee: Why can't it be right, ma'am?

Customer: Because that would mean I'm stupid.

Employee: *Quiet*

Customer: I gotta go. *Hangs up*

Employee: I'm sorry, ma'am, you are a few dollars short of getting the in-store coupon.

Customer: Well....do something about it!

Employee: *Confused on what exactly she is supposed to do about it* Um....well, you can buy another item to get to the minimum.

Customer: *Storms off, returns with a tank top.* Get me this in a medium.

Employee: I can't leave the register, and everything we have is on the floor.

Customer: Well, what am I supposed to do??

Customer: Does this perfume smell old to you?

Employee: No, I like it. It's fresh and smells young.

Customer: Good. I don't want to smell like an old lady's douche.

Employee: *Silent*

Employee: Bye ma'am. Have a good one!

Customer: *Stops* What do you mean by that?

Employee: *Flustered* I just meant...have a good day.

Customer: I don't understand what you mean by that, have a good one. Have a good one? What does that mean? *Leaves store, mumbling to herself*

Customer: Can I leave my item here by the register?

Employee: Yes.

Customer: Are you sure?

Employee: Yes, I'll watch out for it.

Customer: I still want to buy it.

Employee: Right.

Customer: So I can leave it right here?

Employee: Yes.

Customer: Are you sure?

Customer: Where is the scuba gear?

Employee: Sorry, sir, we don't sell scuba gear here. We are a department store.

Customer: You don't sell scuba gear? Why not?

Employee: Well, normally our customers aren't looking for scuba gear.

Customer: But I am!

Customer: What is the price of this item?

Employee: 17.99.

Customer: 17.99? Why not 18 dollars? Your prices should be round numbers!

Customer: This is terrible customer service! I want to speak to the owner!

Employee: You're in a Mervyn's.

Customer: So?

Employee: So there is no Mr. Mervyn you can talk to.

Customer: Is this the pet-special vacuum?

Employee: Yes, this one is especially for pet stains.

Customer: Good. We have a lot of dog vomit at home.

Employee: We can recycle that bag for you if you put it in the bin next to the counter.

Customer: I will when you say please!

Employee: *Stares at her*

Customer: You're welcome! *Grabs bag and storms out*

Employee: Hi there sir, thanks for your patience. Did you find everything you were looking for?

Customer: No! I waited in line for twenty minutes, and that's far too long for anyone to wait to buy anything!

Employee: I'm sorry, sir, it's the holidays, and as you can see, all the registers are being used...

Customer: I don't care! I'm not buying anything! You can put this all back yourself. I didn't wait in line for this kind of treatment!

Employee: Um, so you waited in line to tell me that you aren't going to wait in line?

Customer: Yes! *Storms off*

My favorite customers are in the High Suffer/Low Spender category. We are not a full-service store. We don't do alterations, we don't steam your items and we are not personal shoppers. We do not have a full-time certified vacuum specialist for our three types of vacuums. Having said that, I cannot tell you how many times I've been flashed by female customers wanting me to measure their boobs for a custom fitting. On busy days in the Intimates fitting room I feel like I'm standing on Bourbon Street with an armful of beads.

I want all customers to absorb this. Put your eyeballs right up to the page.

YOU CANNOT GET EXPENSIVE SERVICE WHEN YOU ARE BUYING CHEAP STUFF.

Or to rephrase:

IF YOU BUY CHEAP STUFF, YOU WILL NOT GET EXPENSIVE SERVICE.

We are a discount retailer. At any time, my payroll allows for approximately two people on the floor. These two people cover the following departments: Misses Casual, Misses Contemporary, Petites, Women's Sizes, Men's, Young Men's, Juniors, Accessories, Intimates, Housewares, Big N' Tall, Clearance, Shoddy Electronics, Cheap Jewelry, Overpriced Jewelry, Tacky Outdoors Furniture, Bedazzled Handbags, and Shoes. These two people are also underpaid minions (see Chapter 3 - Awful Associates). Therefore, when you interrogate a brain-dead college student about the thread count on a set of twenty-dollar sheets, you will not be receiving the most sophisticated and researched response.

Nordstrom's is able to give brilliant customer service because 1.) Everyone works on commission, and 2.) A T-shirt costs 100 bucks.

Now that you know this, please, do not go shopping this weekend and ask the sales clerk if the blade sizes for the KitchenAid Mixer on sale are 2.5 or 3.5 inches. If you do this, I will have no choice but to put you in this book's sequel: *Rant of a Retailer Part Two: The Curse of the Cantankerous Consumer.*

Another problem I have is with customers who think every store they visit should have every item their little brains can possibly concoct.

"What do you *mean* you don't have maternity sleepwear?"

"I can't believe you don't carry shark aquarium filters."

"Every store should carry space shuttle parts!"

They're always so shocked. They are also convinced that their size is *not* a specialty size. Trust me – size 42-BBB in bras and size 18 Plus Size Short Petite in pants are specialty sizes. We do not have the floor space, the storage space, or the demand to stock every item in every size and every color out there. Go online! Online is perfectly suited for your eccentric weirdo tastes.

Type in the 42-BBB bra that you are buying for your pet shark in his filtered tank, and I promise you there is a BuyBrasForSharks.com website out there somewhere.

On the flip side of the over–specific customer, you have the way–too–vague customer. This is the customer who calls and asks, in all sincerity, if we carry any T-shirts. We are a retail department store. You have a 100% chance we carry T-shirts.

If you ask vaguely if we carry sweaters, I am going to ask you to be an eensy-weensy bit more specific. Do you want women's, men's, or children's sweaters? Small, medium, large, extra large, plus size? Cardigan or pullover? Full sleeve, short sleeve, 3/4 sleeve? Knit or woven? Pockets or no pockets? Belt or no belt? Cotton, jersey, nylon, or wool? Red orange yellow green blue purple brown black grey white pink chartreuse lavender scarlet ochre chocolate cream mauve canary chestnut lime fuchsia goldenrod denim cornflower lemon turquoise tangerine or sunset?

Do you get where I am going here?

The following stories are more true stories from my delightful consumers. Trust me when I tell you they are true - I couldn't be NEARLY this creative.

Line It Up

Long lines are the pet peeve of most customers. No one likes waiting in line, even though it gives you the luxury of uninterrupted Facebook stalking on your iPhone. We have two registers at the front of the store and another register in Jewelry. One of my jobs as a manager on duty is to pace the triangle between the three registers and maintain the lines. I am forbidden to actually get on a register. I am supposed to pull people from the floor (who are often either trying desperately to get tasks done or, in most cases, non-existent).

This. Sucks. Customers glare at you death rays of hate when you walk by, and I can feel their silent inner rage yelling *get over here and start ringing!* I avoid eye contact at all costs and try to look incredibly busy while mumbling into the radio, "Is anyone available to ring? Anyone? ANYONE??"

Once while circling my register route while avoiding the angry old ladies, the walkie crackled to life. "You have a phone call. A customer wants to speak to a manager." For once the phrase was welcome to my ears, as I could avoid the simmering grumpiness of the lines. I swung behind the jewelry counter and picked up the phone.

"This is Macy. I'm a manager, how can I help?"

The woman on the other end was irate. "Your lines are absolutely out of control! You need to get some more people in!"

"I completely understand ma'am. It's very frustrating to wait in line. When were you shopping with us?" I said in a very conciliatory way.

"I'm shopping with you right now! I'm IN line!"

I glanced up and saw a short, fat woman in a sundress glaring at me from the register line. She was calling to complain about the lines while actually in line.

Pictures of You

Several months ago, my boss was patiently explaining to a customer that her return would come back as an in-store credit, not as cash. The woman was having none of it. With venom she demanded to speak with the store manager.

Boss said, "I am the store manager."

He gestured to the wall where his smiling face beamed out below the customer service promise. "That's my picture on the wall," he said with pride. "I've run this store for six years."

The lady glanced at it, undeterred and said, "That's not you. I want to speak to the manager." She looked at him expectantly.

Boss looked at his photo, which had been taken a few months ago, and looked at the customer. What could he even say to that?

He told her the boss was out of the office and would call her. A few minutes after she left, he called her. Lowering his voice to disguise it, he told her he was the manager and explained the same thing he had just explained at the counter. Since she had finally spoken to the boss, she was satisfied!

A Model Idea

After a long day, I heard my favorite phrase again: "A customer wants to talk to a manager." Begrudgingly I walked downstairs and found waiting by the registers a flamboyant man in the purplest shirt I have ever seen.

"What can I do for you, sir?" I asked him pleasantly, preparing myself for an angry outburst.

"Are you the manager?" he asked, like an accusation.

"Yes, I am," I replied, smoothing my hair behind my ears and sighing inside.

"I have something serious to tell you." he said, his arms crossed, reflecting purple upon purple.

Uh-oh. Did one of my 17-year old employees swear at him? Did he slip on an unknown substance in the wood-floored fitting rooms? Is a lawsuit heading my way?

"It's about your models."

I think hard for a second. Our... models? Nope, I got nothing.

"Our models, sir?"

"Yes, your models! The ones in your ads."

"Oh yes, ok....what....about them?"

"They don't smile enough!!!"

I thought hard again. I was a psychology major. Where was the section about dealing with batty gay purple-shirted men?

"I know you are only a store manager. But you need to address this with your corporate office. I mean, look at them! They are scowling! Do I want to buy clothes from an angry model?" Captain Crazy bellowed, waving his hands about dramatically.

I blinked, astounded. "Absolutely not sir. I'll... get right on that."

"Thank you!" He barked, and he walked off in an angry purple-shirted huff, like an irritated eggplant.

Free CAT Scan

"A customer wants to speak to the manager at customer service!" One of my associates sang out on the walkie-talkie on a regular Monday.

I trudged to the back of the store, where I saw a slightly unkempt elderly lady. She looked like a bespectacled Angela Lansbury, with the silhouette of Mrs. Potts from *Beauty and the Beast.* And she looked very panicked.

"So you're the manager? I have something important to tell you." She paused for my full attention, drawing out the suspense. She took a deep breath, wringing her hands.

I waited with trepidation.

"One of your price scanners scanned my eye!"

I looked at her. I waited.

"You mean...one of the price scanners at the register?" I asked.

"Yes!" She exclaimed with horror in her voice.

"Like, one of the red light scanners? That every store has?"

"Yes!" she said, terror mounting.

"One of the price scanners that my associates use every day?"

"YES!" She stared at me, eyes big, waiting for my reaction. Finally, I understood that she was serious.

"Oh no! Are you okay?" I said, trying to be shocked and grief-stricken, doing my impersonation of Bette Midler comforting dying Barbara Hershey in *Beaches*. I have learned over the years that fake empathy now means less paperwork to do later.

She was happy by my reaction. "Well, yes, but I get migraines. I read that a laser eye pointer shouldn't be pointed at the eyes, so when I saw that red light, I was really worried. Should I fill out an accident report? I want to make sure that my health isn't compromised." Worriedly, she wrung her hands further, occasionally brushing her forehead and rubbing her eye as if to wipe away the imagined deep retinal burn of the price scanner. The price scanner that every clerk at every register in every store in America uses.

Doing my best Bette Midler soft-and-soothing voice, I comforted her that, most likely, she would survive this terrible, terrible injury. In the back of my mind, I am thinking above all thoughts, *I do not want to fill out an accident report.* Accident reports require pages of paperwork, and then a hour-long phone call with our insurance company, explaining all the details that you just wrote down on your sheafs of paper. The more false sympathy I can muster, the less likely it is customers will seek revenge on our store by suing. With this thought, I comfort her, patting her hand, calmly assuring her that most likely, there would be no serious effects. She would pull through this.

Nodding her head, she shook my hand and bravely left the store. A true survivor.

It Doesn't Suit Me

Katherine Heigl's twin, well-dressed and stylish, came up to me and politely inquired, "Where are your women's suits?" She looked like she had come from a law office on her lunch break.

I smiled at her with warmth, and went into a well-practiced spiel, "We have some career pieces and a career collection, but if you are looking for professional two-piece suits, you are better off going across the street."

Her eyes dilated and her breath started coming in fast. She began to huff like Kirstie

Alley going up a flight of stairs. "What do you MEAN you don't have women's suits?"

I shrank back. This was the first time I'd had such a reaction to my career-section speech.

"Umm...we just have our career collection. It's right..over...there.." I gestured limply toward the right, hoping to divert the fury I feel is coming.

"This is DISCRIMINATION!" she bellowed, her voice echoing around the Misses department. Other customers jerked their heads up to stare at us as I shrank back even further. "You have MEN'S suits! Where are your WOMEN'S suits?!? Women work TOO, you know!"

Eek!

I am a huge feminist, and she is completely right. But ... we don't have women's suits! I'm sorry! I swear I didn't pick the men's/women's suit sections!

As I always do, I pretended to have an emergency coming on over the walkie, and I made a just-a-sec finger pause gesture while smiling, and dashed to the back of the store, where I hid out for the rest of the hour. This is how I handle most conflict within my store. Eventually Katherine Heigl wandered off to yell at someone across the street.

God is in the Retails

While I was cleaning up the jewelry counter one day, a nice-looking couple wandered up to me. He was elderly, a silver fox, dressed in dockers and a stylish button-down. She was petite, blue-eyed, and in a darling winter dress.

"I'm looking for a diamond ring for her for our 30th wedding anniversary!" said the husband, beaming at his wife.

"Congratulations!" I exclaimed, smiling back at them. "What's your secret? What's your key to a happy marriage?"

The woman beckoned me over and I leaned into her. She pointed at the ceiling. She held one finger aloft, and held the position. I looked up and back at her. Ceiling tiles? Security cameras were the secret to her success?

She spoke one word. "God."

She stood there, smiling at me. I smiled back, beginning to slowly inch backwards.

Weaving her hands in illustration, she went on, "It's like a braid. There's three strands. You, your husband, and God. It doesn't work without God."

I stood there, still smiling, unsure what else to do. Next to us, her husband was smiling happily as well.

"Now, have you found God?" She asked me, leaning forward over the counter. They both waited eagerly for my response, glancing at each other with eager anticipation.

"Ummm...." I trailed, feeling for the counter behind me to make my escape, "I, uh.... oops! I'm sorry, someone just paged me over the walkie!" I pretended to listen to my earpiece, then I dashed to the other end of the counter to frantically make a phone call to my Men's supervisor.

"Hey! I need you to watch the jewelry counter!" I barked at her. After her startled, "Okay," she came over, and I sacrificed my innocent Men's supervisor to be evangelicalized. I hid in the stockroom, where I was safe from being saved.

My husband says I should've responded, "You might be saved, but I can save you some money with our in-store credit card!"

<u>Bad Manager</u>

Our Home supervisor waved both his arms over his head frantically as I was walking by one Tuesday morning. "Can you help this lady, Macy?" he asked, looking concerned, sneaking quick glances at the customer standing at his side.

"Sure!" I replied, buoyantly. I was having a lovely day, a kind of day where I loved all customers and was eager to help. I walked toward the two of them with a lighthearted step. The woman, a larger black woman, waved me to her side. She looked like Oprah, but turned out to not be quite as wonderful as Oprah.

My home supervisor, looking relieved, began to back away. The woman held up an authoritarian finger, indicating he should stay.

"Does this lady know this department?" She asked him, gesturing to me imperiously like a queen to her subjects.

"Oh, yes," he hastened to reassure her. "She's the manager of all apparel." He looked at me with big hopeful eyes. I nodded my head in agreement. The woman looked appeased and waved him off. He retreated eagerly to his sanctuary of frames and rugs.

"Hi, I'd like to find some active wear shirts in these colors." She held up two basic tank tops, one coral, one yellow.

I glanced at the shirts and then replied, "Oh, okay. Active wear is right over there." I pointed across the aisle. "Did you see the yellow shirt on the wall? Would that work?"

She stared at me like I'm the biggest idiot to walk the earth, and lifted up another shirt she had in her hand behind the tank tops. "See this shirt? It's **active wear**. I've already **seen** active wear. Why would you direct me to active wear when I've already been there?!?"

Ummm....sorry?

"OK, well, what about this type?" I gestured to an embroidered t-shirt.

"**No!** I want a simple shirt I can work out in!" At this point we were in the fashion section of the store. I pointed out a few more shirts, which she vehemently disagreed with.

"How about this kind? Is this what you are looking for?" I gestured to a embroidered yellow short-sleeve top. I prayed that it was, because I have no idea what this lady wants.

"So let me get this straight." She said, staring at me, furious. "You brought me over to the dressy side of the store?"

"Well, no. All of this brand is the same, it's not really dressy or not dressy." I explained carefully. I wasn't sure where this animosity was coming from, and honestly, I was scared to say anything at this point.

She cut me off. "You know what?" She snapped, fuming, "I'm better off shopping on my own." She turned on her heel, back ramrod straight, and walked away from me.

I glanced left and right looking for Ashton to tell me I am on Punk'd. Which I wouldn't be because I am not exactly a celebrity. But why else would I be in this bizarre situation? I then chased down my Home supervisor to bite his head off for giving me Evil Oprah.

My boss later tells me she complained to an associate, then to him, and then got the corporate and district manager phone numbers to complain about me.

Because I offered her the active wear department after she said she wanted active wear. Bad Manager!

Sharing is Caring (and Cheating)

Chit-chatting loudly, two women, one blonde, one brunette, in their early thirties sauntered up to my register. I rang up the first woman's items while they continued their conversation about their husbands, ignoring me.

Gesturing at an important point, Laverne then pushed her coupon for 20% off across the counter and I scanned that as well. After processing her credit card and finishing the transaction, it was Shirley's turn. After ringing up her items, I glanced up and saw Laverne hand the coupon she had just used to Shirley, who then placed it on the counter. Most of our coupons are generic, but the highest percent off ones are given to special customers at special times. The highest percent ones are labeled by the name of the customer.

I looked at the name and then at her credit card. The names, of course, did not match.

"Ummm... is this your coupon?" I questioned her, hesitatingly.

"Yes!" She said brightly, not a trace of guilt.

"Oh, okay..." I trailed off, "But... it has your friend's name on it." *And I just scanned it for your friend thirty seconds ago, you big liar.* I thought to myself.

Her eyes narrowed. "We always share coupons." She put her hand on her hip, daring me to say more.

"Spouses can generally share coupons." I said. "Are you two married?"

"No!" Laverne declared, indignant. "We're neighbors! We always see who has the highest coupon and use that one."

Shirley leaned across the counter and stared me down. "We *always* share coupons. You are the first person to ever question us."

I didn't back down. I stared back at her. "I mean, you can tell that this coupon was meant for the person whose name is on it, right?" *It's common sense, you big cheaters.*

Shirley's nostrils flared. She repeated, "Like I said, you are the first person to ever question this. If it's *going to be a problem*, we *don't have to shop here anymore.*"

Since my store lets customers get away with whatever they want, I honored the coupon. The ladies left, happy that they had gotten their way. But let me reiterate the horrible behavior we had just enforced.

She was mad at me because I made her feel bad for using a coupon that was clearly not meant for her. She felt she had every right to use her friend's coupon. Crazy *and* conniving. Two for one!

Going Postal Over Pillows

A younger woman came in and was looking through our decorative pillows. She brought a couple of red ones up to the price checker, and they scanned at 40% off instead of 50% off. She then proceeded to FREAK OUT.

My poor cashier, whom she was screaming at, was terrified and paged me to the rescue. Tall, mellow Chuck behaved like he ate opium poppies for breakfast, so in his placid state he didn't know what to do with a hysterical pillow lady. I walked quickly to the dec pillow aisle and asked, "Hello ma'am, how can I help you?"

Let me sum up what she said.

"I can't believe this you always do this to me why can't you sign properly I've never had a good experience with this store what is wrong with you people your people are incompetent and I am **NEVER COMING BACK HERE AGAIN!!!**"

I say, "Ma'am, is there anything I can do to ----?" I couldn't even finish the sentence before she roared, **"NO!"**

So what did I say to salvage this relationship and retain a customer, bringing her back into the fold and perhaps earning my company thousands more dollars over the years?

I said. "OK. Bye." And I walked away.

Her jaw dropped down to her knees as she watched me walk away. She caught her breath and opened her mouth to scream after me, "How dare you! You can't do that to me! It's your *job* to help me!"

I didn't give her the finger, but I came close. My middle finger twitched with the urge like an impatient hummingbird.

My store is all about customer service and helping customers. There were tons of things I had the power to do. I could have discounted her pillows to the right price. I could have fixed the sign in front of her. But there are some people that are unsalvageable. She didn't even let me offer to help. The lady was totally done with us, so I was just not going to waste the energy. I kept on walking, head held high, back into the office, while her yells and curses faded away behind me.

Call Me Maybe

One night the phone rang in the office while I was devising ways to avoid the Internet blockers.[1] I answered with my automated perky answering spiel while clicking on various internet settings. "Thank you for calling, this is Macy, how can I help you?"

A young man's deep voice said, "Yes, can I speak to Holly please?"

We discourage private phone calls for our associates. Partly because we don't want them

---

[1] We weren't allowed to ever use Google on company computers, so I was constantly finding ways to get around it so I could job search online during conference calls. I first used Bing, then they banned it, then I move to AltaVista, they banned it, and I moved to WebCrawler. Yes! WebCrawler still exists!

being distracted when they are cleaning up the floor, but partly for their protection. Bill collectors like to call people at work because some associates are adept at avoiding them at home, and estranged, bitter exes liked to trap them on the floor as well.

"Yes..." I said with caution, "May I ask who's calling?"

"No."

Just like that.

"Ummm... hold on." I said.

Taken aback, I paged Holly on Line 2. "Hi honey, there's a guy on the phone for you. He sounds a little sketchy. Do you want to take it?"

Holly is a darling college student with long black hair and sweet face. She was one of my favorites, as she had endless energy and was always happy whenever I saw her. She replied with hesitation, "Um, no, I'll get it." We said good-bye, and I watched the blinking light for Line 1 turn solid as Holly picked it up.

Later that night, I asked Holly, "So who was that on the phone?"

Breaking into giggles, she said, "It was one of the customers from earlier today! He was calling to ask me out!"

Her-story

Customers adore telling us their life stories, most of the time unprompted. One afternoon I helped a woman find a mascara for forty-five minutes while she told me every single aspect of her life. So you can enjoy what I got to enjoy, let me present to you Patty Robinson's life story. Picture me mmm-hmming now and then, but definitely not talking. There was no room to interject any comments in the Patty Robinson Life Story Monolog. I printed some receipt paper and took notes.

"I'm buying this makeup for myself. My husband died three years ago and I'm just getting back into the dating pool. It took me awhile to start over because I was traumatized because my husband died in bed with another woman. Turns out she was his other girlfriend and he'd been dating her for five years. We had been married for thirty-five years! Can you believe that? She's fighting me over the will. We're still in court about it; my lawyer thinks we'll win. So I haven't had time to date. I thought about Internet dating, but I have a friend who got stalked by one of those guys and was almost murdered. So I need a makeover to get ready to date again. I really need to get my hair done. See my nails? I'm going to get a manicure for the very first time ever. I've always lived on a farm so it was never necessary. My daughter is going to take me to the manicurist. She's not bringing her girlfriend. She just came out last year. My son is a real estate agent. He hasn't been back to the farm in years...."

And it went on, and on, and on. Let me remind you this is absolutely a true conversation, her random subject changes are exactly as random as they sound, and this happens to us *all the time.*

Ad It Up

Last week, I had another angry lady (surprise!) She was irate that we didn't have what we advertised in the ad. She launched into an angry tirade on how we could possibly not have the giant yellow anti-gravity chairs corporate posted in the ad. The fact was, we hadn't received them yet and the ad had just gone out that morning. The ads serve every store in the country, from the cold-weather stores to the extra-hot-weather stores. Some locations get more stock than others, and we have no control over what inventory we receive. It's a fact of retail.

I feel about the ads the way I feel about bicyclists. When I am in a car, I HATE bicyclists. When I am bicycling, I HATE cars. It is a complete and total double standard that I realize but will not be changing anytime soon. When I am a customer, I HATE that they don't have what's in the ad. When I am the retail manager, I think "Come on! Chill out! How can every single store have every single product?"

I turn to cyclist mode and sympathize with the lady. After smooth-talking her for a while, I've got the situation totally under control. I've helped her find another type of furniture! She's happy! I am the queen of the retailers!

The next day my boss tells me she has filled out a complaint form about my unhelpful behavior.

Sigh.

It's a Shoe-In

An angry man came up to our return center. He had a pair of ratty, beat up, disgusting old loafers. He had clearly been wearing these shoes day in and day out for weeks.

Loudly, he said, "I've had these loafers for only (*only*!) six months. They've fallen apart, and I want to return them."

My return person said cheerfully, "Absolutely! Do you have a receipt?"

"No." he replied, staring her down.

Helpful Employee said, "OK! Do you have a credit card? Something where we can look up the transaction?"

"No. I bought them with cash."

Now the trouble with cash is that there is no record. This is excellent for criminals who are trying to escape to foreign countries, but very bad for retailers trying to figure out how much customers paid for loafers.

The employee told him our policy, "Well, with no receipt we give in-store credit for the price on the floor. The trouble is we can't tell how much you paid for the shoes, so we give you what the floor price is."

Angry Man started to huff. He started to puff. Angrily, he said, "I want my money. Any other store would give me back my money!" He placed both hands on the counter and leaned forward like he was going to jump across the counter.

This is where our return girl, panicked, called for reinforcements. My boss Donny came out of the office. The entire conversation was repeated again. Donny reiterated the same speech the employee gave. Peeved, Angry Man stormed off!

The coast was clear for a while. But we were not free of Angry Man. Oh no. He popped back up to the counter a few minutes later, slammed his hands on the counter, and petulantly asked Donny, "Do you have my money now?"

Donny said flippantly, "Oh, do you have your *receipt* now?"

Angry Man screeched at this sass, "No! I want my money! Any other store would give me back my money!"

Donny, calmly, like a steadfast rock in an irrational river, asked, "You tell me ONE store. ONE store that would give you your money back."

Angry Man thought, tapping his fingers in irritation upon the wood counter, and, inspired, said triumphantly, "Walmart!"

Donny, undeterred, said, "Fine. Let's call them." He pulled out a phone book from under the counter. He flipped through the tattered pages, running his finger under the W's.

Angry Man turned pale and stuttered, trying to decide what to do. He knew as well as we did that Walmart was not about to give anyone cash without a receipt, and he didn't want the proof that Donny's phone call was sure to uncover.

So while Donny picked up the phone and began to dial, Angry Man came to a decision. He THREW THE SHOES AT DONNY'S HEAD, turned furiously and stomped out. Donny ducked the shoes while cradling the phone as the nasty loafers hurtled into the wall, then yelled at the guy's retreating back, "THANK YOU! HAVE A GREAT DAY!!"

This is the boss that I love. There's nothing more enjoyable than calling a crazy's bluff. Angry Man had been stopped in his angry tracks.

Customers are not only crazy. They're also gross. Throughout the years I have cleaned up countless spilled coffees, half-drunk Jamba juices, and ground-into-the-carpet cookie crumbs. I've found used tampons wrapped in underwear still with tags on it (they all went straight into the trash. Sorry, Hanes vendors!) I have cleaned up vomit-stained clothes from the fitting rooms and pee from the elevators. I have seen a woman wipe her nose on one of our display shirts. But the best/worst disgusting story of my retail experience happened, luckily, to the worst person I ever worked with.

It's Not Just a Job - It's a Doody

So this awful coworker of mine -let's call her SuperSlut. No, no, that's too mean.

We'll just call her Backstabbing B*tch.

BB dashed up to me in the office. I was glancing through the merchandise book, studying the new trends for March (Florals! Lace! Skirts!)

"Macy," she said, her eyes wide and terrified. "I need help."

These were very uncustomary words to come out of her mouth. Generally BB was either a.) Sleeping with her supervisor (he ended up being transferred), b.) Snapping at customers, or c.) Trying to get one of us fired. She rarely would admit to the fact that I was indeed her boss, so it was exciting to hear her plea.

Especially considering what happened next.

Apparently BB was recovering t-shirts in Misses when an overweight, elderly lady came up to her. BB turned to her, when the lady blurted out, "I'm going to have an accident." BB froze– did she mean what she thought she meant?

"Ummm…" BB stammered, "Can I help you get to the restroom? It's right down the aisle here."

The woman waved her arms manically. "There's no time!" she shouted in a panic.

Customers whipped their heads around to stare at BB who returned their glances, mortified.

"Uh, okay, what can I do for you?" BB tried to herd the lady up the aisle to the bathrooms, in a weird, off-balance stance that came from gesturing with her arms while keeping her body as far away as possible from the lady, who was starting to emit an aroma. She looked like an off-balance meerkat escorting an incontinent hippo.

The lady hobbled in the direction BB was indicating, but she wasn't going to make it. Small drops of brown started squirting out of the back of her pants legs, leaving a Hansel and Gretel-type trail, if you substituted bread crumbs with poop crumbs.

BB shared desperate glances with the other associates on the sales floor, but hell if any of them were going to help her. BB had two things going against her:

1.) She was trailing a poopy lady down the aisle.

2.) She was a mega-b*tch.

These two factors contributed to the associates suddenly remembering the ultra-important task they had to do in the Bedding section. At the opposite end of the store.

Poopy Lady made it to the bathroom in her slow, wobbly gait. BB followed her in, where she proceeded to hear an explosion on par with the eruption of Mount St. Helens. Holding both hands over her face to block the smell, she proceeded to start backing out of the smelly bathroom.

"Wait!" Poopy said, beseechingly. "I need help! Please, will you go and get me another pair of pants?"

"Uhmhum, shure," BB said, muffled by her sleeves covering her face. "Illberightback."

She dashed to the office, which is where I came in.

"OK, Sandy," I said. (Oops! Did I just say her real name? *Note to self* - be sure to have Backstabbing B*tch's/ SuperSlut/ Five-Kids-With-Three-Dads' real name edited out). "Here's what you'll do. Go get a pair of clearance pants, five bucks or less. Throw them over the stall to her, with a plastic bag for the nasty ones. Then run away. I will tell Loss Prevention they were stolen."

BB gave me a look of deep, heart-rending gratitude. "Thanks, boss," she said warmly. She started to walk away, an extra spring in her step.

"Oh, and Sandy?" I added.

She turned to me with a beaming smile.

"Clean up the poop in the aisle. Housekeeping's not in yet."

That command was probably the most petty and vindictive sentence I've ever spoken. Some people say being petty is a negative character trait. They say it is only a temporary high, that long-term, I will feel guilty for being such a jerk.

They're full of it. It's freaking great.

By the way, after pooping their pants in a major retail store, most people would probably go home as soon as possible. Oh, no. Not Poopy Lady. NOT ONLY did she continue to shop, she ended up checking out at our registers: one hand full of merchandise to buy, the other hand holding a bag of poopy pants.

We figured it was her master scheme to get free pants. So here's the valuable tip of this chapter- if you want free pants, follow this easy formula:

1.) Go into your local department store.

2.) Poop your pants

3.) Ask for free pants.

If I may speak for the general retail management population, we will give you what you want. I'm sure it's in an Employee Handbook somewhere. If not, I recommend an HR director get on that.

Love at Second Sight

My most triumphant crazy customer care tale took place just recently.

A little background - we make mistakes at our store. All the time. We have over a hundred people in our store, and like any company, communication is our biggest hurdle. One year miscellaneous associates sold our one (1) display gazebo to five (5) different people. It was a sad, sad day when they all came in to try to buy it.

My triumphant tale began with a similar situation. One evening over the walkie I heard, "There's a customer here who wants to speak to a manager!" I trudged unwillingly up front to find an irate Iranian man.

"Where is my ottoman?" He demanded to know as I walked up to the register, his grey unibrow twitching like a squirrel tail. I hate walking into the middle of a situation with zero knowledge. I feel like Snooki entering a White House briefing.

"Sorry sir, can you catch me up? What ottoman?" I asked.

"We called in for an ottoman! It was supposed to be on hold! Now this stupid girl tells me this ottoman belongs to someone else!" He pointed at my cashier Amber, who looked at me, terrified.

"Chris brought the ottoman up here," she explained, "but the hold slip has somebody else's name on it."

I examined the slip. I remembered overhearing the Home employee putting it on hold a few days ago. "I apologize, sir. It looks like this was indeed sold to somebody else."

He drew in his breath, and I braced myself. "What the f*** do you mean, you sold it to somebody else?!?" he exploded.

Oh no. No he didn't.

I can tolerate a customer's abuse - until I hear profanity. Then my feet go out, hands go on my hips, and I stare them down with the wrath of Khan (if Khan was an underpaid blonde woman).

"Don't you dare take that kind of language with me, sir!" I growled in a furious Sauron voice. He blinked and step back a bit. "Now, you wait here. I'll see what I can do." Scowling at me, he complied.

I searched all our local stores through the computer. I found two of the same ottomans in a store in Portland, about ten miles away. Quickly I called and had them put both on hold. The associate assured me, on pain of death, that this specific ottoman would be at customer service.

"Okay, sir, I found two of the same ottomans in our Portland store. The items will be waiting for you at customer service. Here's the address." I told him, handing him the address slip I had hand-written and silently praying to avoid another outburst.

Angry Iranian man transformed instantaneously into a glowing, peaceful angel. I watched him physically transmogrify from Darth Vader into an Ewok.

"Thank you so much!" He gushed, shaking my hand warmly, "Two is even better! You are so wonderful! I will come back here all the time, just for you!"

He rushed out of the store, off to pick up his ottoman and possibly terrorize the other store's associates. Amber and I shared a look of tentative relief.

Now my Iranian Angel comes in all the time. He searches me out, roars excitedly when he finds me, and grabs my hand for an enthusiastic hand-pumping.

From an angry customer to my BFF. All in a day's work.

You've Got to Give Them Credit

Even though we have the evil customers, my adorable customers make my work worthwhile. On a freezing cold December evening, I was rubbing my hands together to keep warm while giving a strained huddle. "OK team, we are very, very behind on credit." I told them, trying not to show my serious concern. "Credit is your number 1 priority! Everyone got it?" This meant hassling our customers to open in-store credit cards. These customers very rarely want in-store credit cards, and they do not enjoy being hassled. It's a win-win situation.

They all nodded, unenthusiastically, and trickled off to their departments. The reason for my panic was the district manager had called me that morning and told me, in no uncertain terms, that we had to hit credit goal that day. As in - I would have to answer to him if we failed. My DM is a super nice guy, except when he is being straight-up terrifying. I would more willingly get a facial from Freddy Krueger than call Darren when he's mad.

So I paced the front of the store, occasionally lunging after customers and grabbing their shirts with a panicked plea to open a credit card. Since people generally appreciate desperate clutching even less than they appreciate being hassled at registers, I did not open any cards. The rest of my team started to pull in a few here and there, my jewelry associate got two, and finally - finally! We were one away from goal!

Which is where we stopped.

For four hours.

I kept up my frantic pacing and clutching, waiting and hoping for that credit bell (a little ding-ding we played overhead when we open a card). Nothing. My terror mounted as I started rehearsing my phone call to Darren. If he yelled at me I was going to throw the phone down, run out of the store, take a flight to a small tropical country with only mini-seashell-selling stores and no corporations, and live on the beach foraging for sand crabs. That was pretty much my plan.

In the midst of my freakout, a big redneck guy and his girlfriend sauntered up to me. His belt buckle was bigger than the Rio Grande. "Hey there, can you show us these earrings?" the woman asked, gesturing to the jewelry counter behind me. "No problem," I said, the strain evident in my voice. "Come on over."

The woman peered into the case. "Aw, honey, I love these!" she cooed at her man. "Well, let's get them!" he said enthusiastically. She pointed at another pair, "But these are lovely, too." "Let's get both of them!" the guy said happily.

I smiled, my strain slipping a bit. Very cute.

"We'll get both of them." Redneck told me. I rang them up, and took my cue to deliver the credit card message. "It's such a good deal, you get discounts all year long, you will love it, do you shop here a lot?" Redneck laughed. "No way. I don't need any credit cards."

Sorrowfully, I put the jewelry into his bag. Redneck noticed my dismay. "Well, now, honey, will you get something if I open this credit card?"

"Yes," I said sadly, "My district manager won't yell at me."

Redneck pulled out his wallet. "OK. Let's do this then."

Shocked, I stared at him. "You're opening a card you don't need so my DM doesn't yell at me?"

"Yup!" he said, winking, with a bright white smile. "I got your back, girl."

In that moment, I have never loved a man more. (Apologies to my husband.)

In summary - my crazy customers both keep me in business and keep me full of choice stories to tell my friends during Happy Hour, while the good customers keep me sane. And yes, if you can remember a time in the past when you went a little nuts in a major department store, we DID make fun of you behind your back. But at least we didn't write it down and make a book out of it or something! Haha!

Oh wait.

Chapter 2

Awful Associates: Surprise! $8.25 an Hour Does Not Buy the Highest Quality Team

"In a hierarchy, every employee tends to rise to his level of incompetence."
-Laurence J. Peter

My employees. My employees are possibly the most random, rag-tag, whiny, high-maintenance, demanding, and annoying group in the country. We have all races, all languages, people over 70, 17-year-old kids, oodles of students, two people with Down's Syndrome, and a one-armed man (who outperforms the two-handed people 99% of the time).

Some of them are amazing. Some of them are retail champions who care deeply about cleaning up the store for the customers. Some of them are dynamic organizers who prepare, to the tiniest detail, for every potential sale. Some of them are capable, competent, hard-working, bright, friendly, and industrious.

And a lot of them are **not.**

Bottom line is, we pay our people minimum wage. A good raise for an employee, on a good year, would usually be...18 cents an hour. The freight supervisor at one of my stores worked for the company for *thirteen years.* His pay?

$13.65 an hour.

Now, there have been numerous recent studies showing that pay is not the most important tool for employee retention. More importantly is praise from immediate managers, attention from leadership, and a chance to lead projects or task forces.

But even with those incentives, it is hard to attract high-quality workers at minimum wage. You get your bored stay-at-home moms, your high-school and college students, your retired grandmas and grandpas, and a *whole* lotta people who have been unemployed for quite a while. Usually for a reason.

When the economy went downhill we received numerous applications from a lot of qualified people. However, those qualified people left us the minute they got full-time, better-paying jobs.

My point is, you can find great people anywhere. But it's easier to find them outside of a store.

So how do I find my winners?

Let me tell you one thing - it's not from interviews. There have been several studies done that indicate that you simply cannot predict from an interview how a person will perform on the job. Not to mention, 78% of managers who use panel interviews in recruitment do not find them indicators of future success.

I hired two candidates when I was first put in charge of hiring. The first one was a college-educated, intelligent (not to mention buff) dude who resembled Channing Tatum. Channing interviewed beautifully, getting the green lights on every question. The other man I hired...well, let's just say when he entered the room for

Orientation, one of the supervisors pulled me aside and asked me if he was homeless.

So go ahead and guess who was with us three years later, moving up through the ranks to become the shoe supervisor and one of our all-time best employees. Through my dramatic use of foreshadowing, I can tell you know it wasn't Channing. No, unfortunately, Channing was caught by Loss Prevention as he was stealing sterling silver on his way out the door.

On the way out from Orientation.

On the other hand, Homeless Paul turned out to be one the best hires I ever made, an efficient, competent, hard-working member of the ad set team. And yes, we did really call him that.

Age makes no difference either. I've had 70-year-olds who could outperform any of my young'uns, merchandising a truck faster than a caffeinated cheetah. The 17-year-old kids can go either way. They are either so impressed about working at their first company they work their tails off, or they don't understand how work is supposed to work and consequently forget to show up.

Here are the following true quotes from my little angels:

Customer: Please help us! My wife tripped on the curb outside and hurt her ankle!

Employee: Yeah. Old people are always tripping on those curbs.

Customer: My daughter is in that dressing room! I can't believe male employees can go inside!

Employee: That's funny, that's the third complaint about that I've gotten today. *Whistles and continues on his way into the dressing room*

Employee: Was there anything wrong with these items?

Customer: No, they were just too expensive.

Employee: Oh, were they a gift?

Customer: No, I bought them. I mean really, who would be dumb enough to pay $16 for towels?

Employee: Well... YOU did.

Customer: I'd like to buy these earrings.

Employee: Oh, no, don't get those. They look terrible on you.

Customer (On Black Friday): Look at these lines! Why are these lines so long?

Employee: *Nastily* Because a lot of people are here.

Customer: This is ridiculous. I can't believe how terrible your customer service is. I'm not going to shop here anymore!

Employee: *Irritably* Please don't!

Customer: That was supposed to be on sale!

Employee: No, ma'am, the item is ringing up full price.

Customer: Well, this dress was on the 80% off rack!

Employee: I'm sorry ma'am, our clearance prices are priced as marked.

Customer: It was on the 80% off rack! It should be 80% off!

Employee: You know, ANYONE could have put that on the 80% off rack. *Takes a dress from the closest rack and puts in on the 80% off rack* Look, magic! It's 80% off!

Employee: I'm going on break.

Manager: What? Who gets a break around here?

Employee: ... Ooo! Pick me!

Customer: So I need to put my annual income in here for this card?

Employee: Yes. It's probably a million dollars, so you should adopt me! Hahaha!

Customer: I do make a million dollars a year.

Employee: Oh. *Pause* ...will you adopt me?

Customer: Is it okay if I bring in this bag? I have my receipt.

Employee: Um, no. Security will think you are a thief.

Customer: Excuse me, do you sell plus-sized lady's clothes?
Employee: No...but SlimFast is on Aisle 10.

Customer: Wow, looks like a really busy day. You all look exhausted.
Employee: Yeah, I hate working here.

Customer: Can I check out here?
Employee: No, this is only for returns.
Customer: But I only have a few items and you don't have a line...
Employee: But if I help you, then I could *get* a line. So no.

Employee: Hi there, can I interest you in a credit-
Customer: NO!

Employee: Do you get our coupons-

Customer: NO!

Employee: Would you like a receipt-

Customer: NO! Just scan my stuff, and do it NOW!

Employee: OK, let me scan your card. *beeps* I'm sorry, sir, it's been denied.

Customer: Oh, crud, I forgot to pay that card off. Do you take Discover cards?

Employee: NO!

Here is a quote from an employee that didn't actually happen but I wish it did. We were discussing a rude woman from another country who was demanding an item we didn't have. The first part of this conversation is true. The last part I wish was true.

Customer: You get me this! Bring it to me in gold!

Employee: We don't have that in gold.

Customer: You are a rude girl!

Employee: *upset* I'm sorry ma'am, we just don't have it.

Customer: You get manager at once!

Manager: What's the problem, ma'am?

Customer: She won't get me this in gold.

Manager: We don't have it in gold.

Customer: You are all rude! You will get this for me!

Manager: I'm sorry, do you speak English? Should I get an interpreter? I'll try to find somebody who speaks B*tch.

The end of this conversation didn't happen, mainly because we don't like waiting in unemployment lines. But the following are true-life stories of my employees. Every day I get to deal with an overwhelming lack of common sense.

<u>Attention to Retail</u>

My employees don't put a whole lot of thought into their work. They get on a groove and just... keep going. One day, I pulled a rolling rack of shirts up to an employee. "Brendan, can you go ahead and hang these?" I asked him.

"Sure thing, boss," he replied cheerfully. Normally, we pull off the sizing stickers when we hang items, so that's just what Brendan did. 300 T-shirts and three hours later, I walked up to him and let out a shriek.

What's wrong?!" asked Brendan, panicked, spinning around to face me, his arms akimbo, like a startled monkey.

"Brendan, what's wrong with this picture?" I asked, irate.

Brendan leaned into the tees, studying them from all angles. He picked up one of the shirts and leaned in for a closer look. Tilting his head to his side, he puzzled over what be wrong with his handiwork. Suddenly seeing the glaring problem, he paled.

"The size sticker had the price tag on it," he whispered mournfully.

"The size sticker had the price tag on it," I repeated.

Without the price tag, there is no way for cashiers to scan the items. Considering he was a full-time cashier, he was pretty aware of this fact.

Brendan was a sad boy that night when he re-ticketed 300 t-shirts.

Paging All Pedophiles

Oftentimes, children get lost in our store. Parents leave their children in the toy section (or as we like to call it, daycare) and wander away. This leads to sticky 5-year-olds coming up to the front and crying to the cashiers.

One time, a sweet new cashier, being helpful, paged overhead, "Can Tommy Stewart's parents please come meet him at the left registers? Tommy Stewart's parents to the registers please!"

Let me translate this page for you.

"Can all available pedophiles please come to the left registers? All available pedophiles who want to abduct a child to the registers, please!"

When I heard this over the intercom, I lunged desperately towards the nearest phone, called the extension, and screamed over the phone at the associate. "Why are you trying to kill me?? Don't get our customers' kids stolen from our store!!"

Get them stolen in someone else's store.

Preggers

Some of my employees are of the Teen Mom variety. I worked in one store where at least five associates were pregnant on a rotating basis. As soon as one gave birth, the next was pregnant. We had one employee whom I did not know when she was not pregnant. Literally. I met her when she was pregnant, then she went out on maternity leave, and when she came back she was pregnant again.

For three years in a row.

Needless to say, they are all under 21 and none of them are married. I would not judge this, except they are working in retail for 9 dollars an hour, ten hours a week, and supporting a family by themselves. How far does 360 dollars a month in salary go?

Not far enough for birth control, apparently.

Pink About It

One of our supervisors had a tendency to call out every 5th day. We have an attendance policy (kind of), but she was BFFs with the boss, so she coasted by. Every time she would call out my blood would boil. Especially because technically, SHE was in charge of attendance.

Since she called out for every slight cough and bruised bump, you can just guess the day she decided to suffer through her illness and come to work.

When she had freaking PINKEYE!

Pinkeye is so insanely contagious, I am scared to type the word "pinkeye" down for fear little pinkeye germs can spawn and mutate from the written word. I would not put it past them.

We are in a community office. Everyone shares desks, phones, and pens. Pinkeye colonies formed on every available surface in my office. I attached Purell to my belt and wiped down highlighters before I used them. And of course, we all came down with pinkeye.

O Captain, my Captain

As a professional, I follow the uber-important rule of being respectful to my boss. Even when my boss was the most condescending, incompetent, patronizing, unprofessional, useless, ineffective, and pathetic manager since retail began (see chapter 8: The Bad, Bad, Bad, Bad, Bad, Bad Boss), I showed a deferential attitude. People promote people they like and trust, and the quickest way to derail my career is to have a negative relationship with the person in charge of my promotion.

Some people do not share the same outlook.

Kaylee, my Misses supervisor, was such a case. Kaylee had been angling to move up in the store for months, but she had one thing holding her back: her terrible temper. Kaylee argued with customers, argued with associates, and argued with managers.

Why did we keep her? She was a kick-ass merchandiser.

Kaylee was also one of those sweet-to-your-face, evil-behind-your-back girls. She would write me a long love letter extolling my virtues as her manager, and then complain bitterly about me behind my back. Round-faced, with a long brown ponytail and sweet brown eyes, Kaylee came off as lovable as a My Little Pony, but secretly hid the personality of Cruella DeVil.

On a cold March day, I strode up to Kaylee and said in a jovial tone, "What are you up to?" gesturing at her handiwork. She showed me the project she was working on, I offered some advice, and I went on my way. Later that day my boss called me in for a sit-down, where I was regaled with the evil I had committed. Apparently, Kaylee was furious that I had the balls to ask her what she was doing.

Let me translate Kaylee–language for you:

What I say: What are you up to?
What she hears: You don't know how to do your job!

What I say: Are you interested in moving up?
What she hears: You don't get a promotion unless you obey my commands!

What I say: Your hair looks cute today!
What she hears: I hate you and want to destroy you and my master plot will come to fruition bwah-ha-ha-ha-ha!

Okay, those were jokes. Kind of. I really don't know what she thinks, only that she has a patent on misinterpretation. During the remainder of the conversation, she told me that I "freak out too much" and "just need to relax." She went on to tell me that other associates had problems with me, and she was their spokeswoman.

What a noble role she undertook.

The only problem was *I am directly responsible for her promotion*. She *cannot* get promoted without me.

So pop quiz for you: if you want to be promoted, should you criticize and alienate the person responsible for promoting you?

Here's the answer again, if you weren't sure: NO.

In *Games Mother Never Taught You*, Betty Harragan states, "*absolute deference to the authority invested in your immediate boss* is the undeviating Number One Rule of the game." (Italics mine) The book theorizes that work is a game, with teammates and captains and rules. Harragan asserts that some women have not learned how to play the game properly. The most important rule is to defer to your boss, even if you disagree. If your boss sucks, you switch bosses. But you do not directly defy or criticize your leader. It's against the rules of all sports teams and the military hierarchy.

And it does NOT lead to promotions. You hear that, Kaylee?[2]

Customers Crazy, Employees Lazy

It blows my mind how lazy my team can be. They put great work and effort into being lazy. Like the Weasels (see Chapter 13: Loss Prevention, or Don't Steal), if they put that effort into actual work, my store would make about a billion dollars a year. I've heard rumors of associates leaving the store and going to see a movie in the middle of their shifts, since it is hard to track their movements throughout a 100 thousand square foot store.

Barry, one of my cashiers, was that kind of lazy. Barry was as lazy as a sloth on downers. I would introduce him to new managers as Barry-He's-So-Lazy. "Oh, that guy? That's Barry - he's so lazy."

Barry would stand at his register and stare ahead of him, mouth ajar, like a stoned goldfish. For *hours*. Most people during down time would clean up around them, straighten the racks, size

---

[2] In case you were wondering, Kaylee did not move up in our store. She stormed out of the job one day after fighting with a customer. *Shocker.*

some folds. Not Barry-He's-So-Lazy. Barry would patiently stare at the wall ahead of him, interrupted from his reveries only by demanding customers who wanted, of all things, to be rung up.

Want to know how we finally managed to fire him? He had been working some shoe shifts, and we got him for sleeping during his shift in the shoe stockroom. How did we know? We saw a corner of the stockroom had several squashed shoeboxes. He was using the shoeboxes as pillows, and we figured out the indentations were from his head.

Traitors

Not only are my people lazy, they're traitors as well. I will never forget Katie, the young, single mother who worked my Juniors department. Katie asked me to write a letter of recommendation to the court system so she could keep full custody of her child. I wrote a glowing letter, expanding on her dependability, work ethic, and sense of responsibility. I cited the years I had worked with her and what I had seen her accomplish. I raved over her capabilities and determined attitude, describing her as a modern Joan of Arc, only she battled unfolded clothing instead of the English. I signed and dated it, and was prepared to go to court as a character witness.

After the trial date, Katie came to me, elated. She had full custody of her child! I hugged her with warmth and told her how proud I was. She beamed at me and thanked me for everything I did for her.

Three months later, the district manager pulled me into an office and said Katie was instigating complaints against me in an effort to get me fired, because she blamed me for the lack of hours she was being scheduled.

Loyalty has a short memory.

Inspiration by Irritation

I pride myself on my evening huddles. Huddles are when you gather around your troops and give them the rundown on the store, any special sales, our credit card incentives, and any fun activities we have planned for the week. I am a rah-rah girl to the max, shaking my retail pom-poms with almost every sentence. "So yay! We have a baby sale this weekend! And it's Senior Day! Babies and old people are the best! GO TEAM!!!"

Seriously, this is what my huddles sound like. One night I was really trying to pump up the morale even more than usual. I asked the group what positive stories they had about our company.

Sandra started out eagerly, stepping forward into the middle of the group's circle. "My sister lives in Arizona, and her daughter just had a baby. She registered at our store and got 20% off her entire registry. She was able to buy twice what she needed because the prices were so much cheaper than anywhere else."

Everyone clapped encouragingly.

Kate raised her hand and went next. "I've worked here seven years, and every year I receive a raise. My brother-in-law worked at our neighbor company, and he first had a pay freeze for two years, then was laid off when they did budget cuts! I love this store because I have job security and a terrific team!"

Everyone clapped again, with some of the younger kids cupping their hands around their mouths and adding a *woot-woot!* to the mix.

Then came Ben. Ben was born somewhere around the Mesozoic era. I would not have been surprised to find out he was raised by a pterodactyl. That would explain both his age and his lack of social skills.

Ben began, speaking slowly. "My wife was shopping here the other day. We've been shopping here for as long as I've worked here...oh, must be five years."

People nodded supportively, exchanging satisfied glances.

He went on, "She tried to pay with a check. It was denied. I asked the manager on duty to fix it. He wouldn't. So I asked our store manager. And he refused to help."

Confusion began to murmur in the group.

"There is no reason her check should have been denied. She wrote a check that same day to another store. No one would help her on the floor, not even calling the bank to inquire about it."

"And **that** is why she has decided to never shop at our store again."

Ben finished his story and leaned back on his heels. A few people weakly clapped, then dropped their hands as they exchanged bewildered glances.

I jumped into gear, stepping forward and clapping my hands enthusiastically. "Um ...great! Now get out there and make the magic happen!"

Thanks for the great story, Ben! Way to motivate the team! Only Ben would decide the best time to rant against the store would be during a morale-pumping, team-building huddle. It must be how the pterodactyls raised him.

By the way - his wife was totally back shopping at our store the next week. The check she had written was for over three hundred dollars, which gets flagged at every store. Her next purchase? Paid by credit card.

1-800-I-Hate-My-Boss

The corporate hotline at any large business is completely anonymous. Employees can call at any time to complain, without fear of retribution. I have been on the receiving end of countless calls. The problem with these calls is after I am spoken to, I have to act exactly the same towards the troublemaker, otherwise it's retribution. So after being scolded, yelled at, and humiliated by my boss because of a weenie crybaby associate, I have to pretend I am not furious at the weenie crybaby associate. I have to schedule them the same amount of hours they were getting, I have to smile at them, and above all I cannot avoid them. My natural instinct after being b*tched about is to avoid the b*tcher, but this is forbidden.

I have personally never used 1-800-I-Hate-My-Boss. As I mentioned before, the complaints come back to the boss. The anonymity is promised, but if you give your name, I promise it will come back to the upper management.

Or if you avoid giving your name but then give a super specific example like, " Well, one time my boss and I were standing in front of the Little Girls fitting room on July 10th at two in the afternoon and she said this..." - it's pretty likely that the boss is going to figure out who you are. After all, she was kinda there.

ASM = Atcher Service, Ma'am!

I would like to say that all assistant store managers are as talented, hard-working, and conscientious as you can clearly tell that I am. Alas, this is not the case. Executives have been fired for taking naps in the LP office. One guy left the entire building unlocked overnight, in essence leaving millions of dollars of merchandise exposed and ready for the taking. One store manager called out on Black Friday, the all-time busiest day of the year... *twice.*

Working with the other ASMs, we always have a deep rapport. Only we know the trials of being an assistant store manager. We get constant complaints from below from customers and associates, and constant pressure from above from corporate and store managers. We are expected to implement hundreds of make-associates-happy measures, such as hand-written cute little compliment notes for all 90 of our people, while once a year getting a scribbled "Thanks" from the DM for ourselves. It is a totally thankless job. At least as an associate I would get a candy bar when I do a good job. As an ASM- I don't even get chocolate.

Do I sound totally sorry for myself? Yes. Self-pity is the theme of this book. Enjoy.

Arrested Management

Slightly more than half of retail employees are women according to the National Retail

Foundation. I was shocked by this statistic. I thought it was something like 90%. Or maybe that's just in my store. I have very few male employees as a rule.

As I mentioned earlier, I am a feminist, but I often find it easier to manage men. I can bark orders at men and yell at them when they do something stupid. They will generally agree with me and promise not to do it again. Many women, on the other hand, I have to handle carefully. I have made countless female employees cry for being too direct and critical. My personal record was Sandra, who I made cry within the first three minutes of her very first shift at the store because she was late.

Multiple studies have been done on how women and men differ in the workplace. Women focus more on compromise, men are better at managing up. I have personally found that my women are more detailed and careful, and my guys are more confident and energetic. And like I mentioned before, I can snap orders at my men without hurt feelings. Which I absolutely love to do. "Work harder! **NOW**!"

We're taught as managers to adjust our management style to each associate. My favorite is the spreadsheet they gave us of the quadrants of age and how to manage them. You have to manage the Boomers and the Millennials very differently. The Baby Boomers, born in about 1940-1955, were raised as hard workers with a respect for authority. You tell a Boomer to do it and they do it. It's pretty sweet. Millennials, on the other hand, were born from 1990-2000, and are big annoying self-entitled babies. There is a whole pamphlet about how to motivate Millennials. You have to give them lots of praise and you can't criticize them or they shut down. You have to explain to them *why* they're doing something and the reasoning behind it. So I find myself in the midst of a crazy, frantic, twenty-thousand piece truck process having sit-downs with my new little Millennial, explaining in great detail why we put out freight. *"So you see, Tommy, it all starts with the supply chain and the distribution center..."*

My ideal associate is a 50 year-old guy or older, with a long previous career who is now working part-time for extra cash. This guy is low maintenance and high productivity, and I can yell at him when I want to. So if you are this guy, please read on and apply at my store.

How to Get a Retail Job

If you still want to work in retail (obviously, you have not finished this book yet), here is some solid hiring advice for you. When people are job searching, they are advised to find a manager to give their resume to them in person, usually by asking the manager to be paged to the customer service desk.

Do not do this.

I am running around doing a thousand things. The last thing I want to do is talk to an eager beaver about job opportunities. Recently, I was pulled to the register (across the store from where I was deeply involved in a project) where, "a customer wants to speak to the manager about a complaint."

"Hello, ma'am." I asked truculently, after trudging across the store, leaving my project behind unwillingly, "What is your complaint?"

The woman glared at me and said, "I'm complaining that no one's called me back about my job application."

So, first of all, the fact that the first words out of her mouth are, "I'm complaining," does not bode well for her as an employee. I do not need any more complainers, thanks so much.

(THEN on her application, she wrote her availability as 8am-12pm, Monday through Friday. We are open 18 hours a day, and our busiest times are on afternoons and weekends. Why exactly would we need you for four hours on weekday mornings? Go work for a dentist.)

If you want to give your application to a manager, *go to the manager*. Do not make him or her come to you. Ask the customer service person where in the store the manager is, and head on over. Be appreciative of my time– I don't have a lot of it. Be charming and low maintenance. If you are high maintenance in the first few minutes, I can only imagine what you'll be like over the next year. And do not start your sentence with, "I'm complaining."

If you do all these things and you are available on weekends, I'll be pleased, and I'll offer you an interview. Sometimes I'll offer you a job right off the bat, especially the month before the holidays when we are scrounging for holiday help. I find second and third interviews silly.

You know everything you need to know about somebody in the first five minutes. Malcolm Gladwell in the bestselling book *Blink: The Power of Thinking Without Thinking* states you make up your mind about someone even faster than that - in the first two seconds!

My interview process takes ten minutes or less. Here are my questions:

1.) Do you hate people?
2.) Are you going to steal stuff?
3.) Are you going to be late or call out?
4.) Are you lazy?
5.) Any felonies?

If a person answers no to my questions, they're in! You may ask, but who would say yes to any of these? You'd be surprised. During one of my interviews, the interviewee asked extremely specific questions about our policy on prosecuting shoplifters. When I asked about her interest, she mentioned offhandedly that she was fired from her last job for theft. This is what we call a red flag.

So what do I do with my demanding little brats? My personal rules for retention are:

1.) Don't mess with people's schedules

2.) Don't mess with people's pay

When I follow these rules, I keep my people. At least the ones I want to keep. My bad bad boss used to pride himself on his incredible retention rate. It was something upwards of 80%, which is unheard of in retail. Most people revolve in and out of retail like a fly on a wagon wheel. While he was proud of his retention, I thought it was a terrible thing for our store. If a retention rate is that high, it means nobody is getting fired. And at our store we *needed* to fire people.

Corporations are so scared of litigation now, it takes a twelve-step process to fire an employee who is openly smoking pot on your sales floor. You have to fill out a counseling form, get eight witnesses to document it, and verify the type of the weed on form 9-B. The only way I can really fire anyone is for attendance, so you can be sure I keep careful tabs on it, as do my other managers. One time I came into the office to discover my co-worker doing a happy dance by herself, jigging across the carpeted floor.

"What are you so happy about?" I asked her. She did a cheerleading jump, extending her arms above her head enthusiastically.

"Jared just called out for today! That's number 15!" She squealed.

My heart leapt with joy. "Oh my gosh, hurray! Let's go fire him!" And we grabbed hands and danced through the office to terminate Jared, our chronically incompetent and body-odor challenged floor associate.

That was a joyous day.

It was also a rare one. Our store is so reluctant to fire associates that it took over six months to fire a Beauty associate who had been caught *on videotape* mocking our boss in front of a group huddle by gesturing towards him and *picking her nose*. And STILL we took forever to fire her!

Since it is so difficult to fire people, I have to be more strategic in getting rid of associates I don't want. I use a few tactics. Such as not scheduling them. Ever. Often this does not deter them. We were purposely not scheduling Alice for about a month because she was a terrible employee and we were hoping we could make her quit. I had to explain to her how to fold a T-shirt three or four times before she grasped the concept, and once I had caught her dumping a huge armful of merchandise into a cart and *hiding* it in one of the corner fitting rooms. After a few weeks of not being on the schedule, Alice called my boss and asked what the problem was. Rather than give her the correct explanation, which was: "You are a bad employee," he launched into a jumbled, obscure reasoning about payroll hours. Undeterred, Alice pressed him, "So, I'll be scheduled next week, right?" Cornered like this, my boss had no choice but to say yes.

Well, he did have a choice, but we are not so honest about performance evaluations at my store.

Then my boss caved AGAIN with Stephanie, one of our worst employees. Stephanie was scheduled once every two months at the max, and the few times she was scheduled she gave away her shifts. Every six months I would work with her and look at her in shock, trying to remember her name. "You still work here? Really?" My teammates and I decided the boss needed to have a sit-down with her and talk her into quitting, since clearly she wasn't committed to the job.

Garrett, my co-manager at the time, and I stalked out our boss's office, pretending to work, as he sat Stephanie down for a good, hard discussion. After about twenty minutes, Stephanie came out of his office, red-eyed and sniffling. We looked sympathetically at her, shaking our heads in commiseration as she left the room, then leapt up and ran to our boss's door. "You did it! She's crying! Great work!" Garrett and I high-fived each other with glee. My boss looked shame-facedly at us.

"Actually...." he stammered.

We looked at him. Our high-fives dropped. "No." I said incredulously. "No, you didn't."

My boss stared at the ground. "It's just...she was crying....she says she needs this job...."

I stomped my foot and said angrily, "She works here twice a year! What does she need this job for?" Garrett and I gave him matching glares. I knew I suffered from Cry-And-I-Cave Syndrome but I didn't know my boss did as well.

My boss shrugged sheepishly. "Sorry guys. I added her to the next two weeks' schedule."

So that went particularly well.

Usually employees quit on their own anyway. In retail, usually about half the staff calls it quits every year and is replaced by newbies. I'm always surprised by what we call NCNS - No Call No Shows. There's an actual large section in the attendance handbook on how to handle these. We get so many of them there's a how-to guide!

I would never just not show up for work. Number 1, you can't get hired back by that company again, ever. Number 2, you lose respect from all your managers and co-workers. Number 3, who does that? "I don't feel like working there anymore, but I am not going to call and give two week's notice. I'm just going to .... not go to work."

I know that retail is not the only industry with lazy employees. I know that white collar companies have their share of derelicts, the only difference being they sleep during conference calls instead of in the shoe stockroom, and they get paid thousands of dollars more while slacking.

All I know is that people who come to my store have a 50/50 chance of being successful. My champions make my life easier and my day happier. My slackers make me want to punch them in their lazy little heads. There is no way to have a team where you are perfectly content with every member. All I can do is hold tight to the good ones.... and watch the bad ones' attendance.

Chapter 3

The Music, or, Taylor Swift Has a Permanent Paycheck

"Anything that is too stupid to be spoken is sung."

-Voltaire

I like Taylor Swift. I really do. Who doesn't? She's beautiful and talented, with a cool blend of country and pop. Taylor puts on a great show, plays her own instruments, and writes a line of poetry on her arm before she performs. How unique and trendsetting is that?

Having said that - if I saw her in person, I would break her guitar over my leg and jump on the pieces. Sorry, TayTay.

My store plays every song Taylor has ever written. I hear "Fifteen" fifteen times a day. I hear "Teardrops on My Guitar" in my sleep. Whenever a new song by Taylor comes on the radio I count the days until it's on our playlist. It usually takes about three weeks.

The same goes for Colbie Caillat and Jack Johnson. The Corporation has decided that these artists are the most perfect, non-offensive, yet relatable artists that they could possibly choose. Therefore they play them over and over and over and over and OVER again.

Ronald Milliman reported that supermarket shoppers shopped longer, moved slower, and purchased more when slow tempo music was played compared to fast tempo music. My company has taken this deeply to heart.

So all day every day I hear the Taylor-Colbie-Jack loop. But wait! It gets better! My store has chosen to adapt the style of "Zoning." Zoning tailors the music to a particular area of the store, based on the ideal customer demographic. To keep us relevant and new and super awesome cool, we have DIFFERENT music in the Juniors section. This music is hip-hoppy, fast-paced, on the edge, and picked out by 50-year-old men isolated in a Midwest building.

What this means is when you are working in the middle between Juniors and the other departments, you slowly go insane. Your left ear hears a slow mopey love song, while your right year is inundated with, "It's a DANCE party! You're YOUNG! Spend MONEY!," set to a DJ Pauly D beat.

Coldplay is another victim of the big-box retail music destroyal scheme. I think most people would agree that Coldplay is pretty edgy and cool. They're British! They performed on American Idol! The lead singer is consciously uncoupled from Gwyneth!

However, after hearing Clocks for the 8,000th time, you find yourself wishing that Chris would just go back to naming his children weird food names and get out of music business entirely.

The other thing I have noticed in my store is the prevalence of Christian music. I actually like Christian music regardless of religion, but I am pretty surprised by how often they play it. Most companies strive to avoid any references to religion, ethnicity, gender, or anything that could possibly be considered offensive, so as to not alienate any potential customers. So I'm always taken aback when I hear a song referencing God playing overhead.

They are generally pretty subtle about it. Lots of Christian songs can be inferred to be songs about a lover, not Jesus.

Song Lyrics:

Your love never fails, never gives up, never runs out on me.

You're the reason for every good thing.

You're always right beside me, and I need you now.

See what I mean? You really can't tell those aren't referring to a boyfriend.

Most of the songs they play are like that - not overtly Christian, but more open to interpretation. Most times I won't know it's a Christian song unless I hear it on the Christian radio station or Shazam it.[3] However, we have one song we play during the holidays that blows my mind every time I hear it. An Aretha Franklin-type singer warbles her way through a version of Silent Night. During one of the

---

[3] You need this app, by the way.

musical interludes, the singer suddenly launches into a religious-laden sermon. She says something like this:

On this day, our Lord and Savior Jesus Christ was born. We give praise to God for giving us this tiny baby, who will grow up to be the King of Kings. God bless us all!

Is this … okay? Won't our Hindu customers be a little annoyed? I don't know. The music pickers don't really ask my opinion.

Needless to say, when ANY of these many-played store songs come on the radio, I jab the button to change stations so hard I dislocate my finger. A rabbit with rocket boosters could not move faster than I do when I hear the first licks of "Bubbly." I've almost swerved off the road trying to change the station off of "I'm Yours." The best part about that song is that my store has decided to edit out the naughty words such as "damn" (gasp!) and "god-forsaken" (blasphemy!) (only religious speeches are okay!). They then proceeded to hire some terrible editors, and the song now skips an unwieldy 8-count to overlap the bad words. So the song jerks along disjointedly, disconcerting our customers and giving me an immediate migraine.

Real Song:

It's our god-forsaken right to have love, love, love.

Edited Song:

It's our (whiirrrr, click) our our right to have l-oh-oh-ve, love love.

Can you imagine listening to a distorted version of this twelve times a day?

There is one song, and one song only, that I have heard approximately eight thousand times and am still not tired of. And that song is – "Stuck On You" by Sugarland. Why, you may ask? I have no idea. This is the only catchy little tune that does not drive me out of my mind. Thanks, Sugarland. Keep those songs coming.

I have listened to the same music for five years with one memorable exception. My first year, Corporate decided to switch music vendors. The installers came in, they switched out all the old equipment, pressed play and left. The music was great, lilting and fun, a little different, when suddenly, halfway through our

Saturday afternoon mega-sale, the music switched from gentle and bland pop to hard-core hip-hop. I mean *hard-core*. This was no MTV Music Award Vanilla Ice mix. This was Two Chainz doing George Carlin's Seven Forbidden Words monolog in rap format. There was explicit swearing, shouting, and multiple choruses involving popular four (and five letter) words I cannot write in this delightful, family-friendly book.

This went on for **two solid days**. First of all, my boss wasn't there that weekend, and my co-assistant manager and I thought this was the funniest thing ever and didn't report it until Sunday night. This is one of my greatest retail memories. Garrett and I would gather up front, pretending to help cashiers or count registers, but really we were watching customers come in. It was the same entrance for every customer. Grandma would amble in, make her way to the carts, and push off into the store. She'd make it about ten steps when she would stop and cock her head, listening to the words. Shaking it off in disbelief, she would go a little farther. Another ten steps and she would stop again, listening. Sometimes she would mouth the words in shock. Meanwhile Garrett and I would be clutching each other's hands underneath the registers, trying to keep the other from exploding out in laughter. "Shut up, shut up!" I would whisper to him, snorting with mirth. "No, you shut up, you little...." and he'd say one of the rap swear words and we would collapse on the floor in hysterics as Grandma walked out the door in a huff.

Retail attracts mature employees.

Sadly, they repaired the music. It turned out the new music system had been picking up on a local rap station's radio signal. We were disappointed that Monday when our old soundtrack was reinstated. Not only was the rap music endlessly entertaining, our sales were so low that weekend we got to leave early. It was a double win!

BUT Corporate has this weird thing about not alienating customers. They went back to the same pablum music mix that I have listened to for the last five years. Customers rarely mention the music. They tune it out or only subconsciously absorb the beat. There is only one customer I remember who complained about our musical choices.

Please Hold

While scheduling my next fixture update on the computer, I noticed the customer service phone light was blinking incessantly. I picked it up.

"This is Macy, how can I help you?"

The other end of the line erupted into an angry old lady's squawking. "I've been on hold for five minutes!"

I sighed. "I'm so sorry, ma'am. How can I help you?"

"You can start by changing your hold music!" She barked at me. "You know, lots of your customers don't want to listen to that new hard-rock music. You should talk to whoever's in charge of that."

I apologized again, and helped her find what she needed. After I hung up, curious, I made a call to the store to see what the hold music was. I beeped through the appropriate choices and waited for the hold music to fill the line.

And it was.... Justin Bieber.

Idol Worship

I will end this musical chapter with the story about the only two celebrities I have ever seen in my store, because they were both music-related. Perhaps they had heard about mine and Garrett's rap music weekend and were drawn in. The only two celebrities that have entered in my store were both from the show American Idol.

Right after the sixth season of the show premiered, I was working the Customer Service desk when the walkie crackled to life and my Home associate screeched, "Blake Lewis is in Housewares by the wineglasses!" Blake Lewis was the beat-boxing runner-up to the winner Jordin Sparks that season. My customer service associate and I jerked our heads to look at each other, then stampeded across the store to Housewares like aroused rhinos. Blake was with his girlfriend, apparently shopping for his new house. He turned an aisle corner to smack into a wall of four smiling female associates. Weirded out, he and his girlfriend backed up, and we advanced.

"Hi!" I chirped. "Can we help you find anything?"

"Nooooo....." he said cautiously, "We're just looking." He backed up a little further and we advanced a little further.

"Are you sure?" I asked, wide-eyed and eager. My associates chimed in behind me, nodding their heads in unison to signify our helpfulness.

"Yes, I'm sure," he said. He stared at us, my associates beaming high-powered groupie smiles at him. His girlfriend grabbed his hand behind his back and started pulling him away to the vacuums and they left, both casting anxious looks over their shoulders in case the rhinos advanced after them. We collapsed in giggles. I immediately announced his position over the walkie for the next batch of associates to see him, who in turn trumpeted his movements to the next part of the store. Poor Blake didn't get his shopping done that day. I think he left after about the fifth round of helpful associates found him in Men's Accessories.

The second celebrity was also from Idol, albeit a little less successful. During one of the audition segments, an auditioner gained celebrity status when Simon Cowell observed his enormous eyes and compared him to a bush baby.

We didn't only see this guy in our store–he applied for a *job* at our store! We took turns during the group interview to come in the interview room and look at his bush baby eyes. (Which were amazingly luminous, by the way. We tried to turn off the lights to see if they glowed in the dark, but the lights were automatic and couldn't be overridden). The interviewees must've been surprised that they were interviewed by eight supervisors for two minutes each.

In the end we decided to offer Bush Baby a job. But get this–he turned us down to work for

Toys "R" Us! We can only assume he was more comfortable working with his own kind.

And so I remain in my music-filled store, memorizing all of Taylor Swift's song lyrics and fantasizing about working in a job without a music soundtrack. Like undertaker, perhaps. Instructor to the deaf. Deep-sea diver. Horse whisperer.

Unless the horse is whispering Colbie Caillat.

Chapter 4

The Corporate Problem

"Bureaucracy is the art of making the possible impossible."
-Javier Pascual Salcedo

Every company has a corporate office. Corporate is the main office, the center of the world, the humming, buzzing, whirring, idea machine. Corporate is where sales, marketing, finance, product management, accounting, and merchandising departments all come together to, in concept, set the one unifying vision for the thousands of stores in the world.

The problem you find in corporate is that it is a *whole heckava lot* easier to **make** plans then to actually **execute** plans. Corporate delights in sending outrageous and unrealistic goals for its stores. The problem is, the visual department might not communicate so well to the price changes department, which means both will make a major plan on the same day, requiring 60 people each, when my entire store staff is 80 people.

Corporate also tries to eliminate as many people as possible from the floor before the whole system collapses. It's like Retail Jenga. We used to have a Beauty person, Home person, and Kids person. They got rid of the Beauty position, then combined the Home/Kids person. We used to have 4 managers, and they changed it to 3. Maybe they can make it one. Maybe one person can run a store 18 hours a day, 7 days a week. They're going to give it a try!

We complain a LOT about Corporate at the store level. And we are very adept at distinguishing between the projects that are necessary and the projects that are totally not gonna happen. I can always tell when a new person has joined a certain Corporate team, because the pointless projects increase exponentially. We have a master calendar, and on any given day you can find me happily checking off projects as complete, even when I haven't come close to touching anything related to the project. What you gonna do, Peter Jacobsen, Marketing Team Lead of Hosiery? You gonna come check to see if I colorized your nylons properly? Come on over!

Above all, Corporate loves making us push credit cards. Credit cards are godsends to all department stores because:

1.) They avoid all the major fees from Visa, MasterCard, AmEx, etc.
2.) They can market like maniacs to all customers and send them flyers / coupons / mailings every other day.
3.) They can charge $35 dollar overdraft fees, $25 late fees, and make pure profit on people's basic unwilling nature to pay stuff back.

So it is Corporate's goal to make all the poor underpaid associates sell credit cards every minute of every day. We are trained to ignore when people say no and keep pushing, because 10% of all people will cave when they are bullied.[4] So bully we do.

An article I read detailed a company that coached associates to obtain cards any way possible - even through fraud. "One of my managers told us that when customers wrote checks and produced their driver's licenses for

---

[4] I just made this statistic up. But it seems about right.

proof of ID, that we should note their driver's license number. In many states, they're the same as Social Security numbers," recalls JaLynn Hudnall, a consultant in the Atlanta suburbs who worked at a local chain store back in 2004 .

"Once the customer had left the store, the manager would fill out the credit application with the information from the customer's check. She figured, if they didn't want the card, they could cancel it once they got it in the mail," she says.

I have gotten very, very good at selling our credit card (non- fraudulently, I swear). I'm one of the best in our store. Here are some tips for you poor plastic pushers out there:

1.) **Stalk Your Prey.** You must evaluate your prey with the utmost of care. I can tell within three seconds if my customer is open to hearing about a card. In my opinion, the most open customers are a.) Men, b.) People from outside the US, and c.) Young people. This is not meant to be stereotypical, sexist, racist, agist, or any other -ist. This is only what I have observed, for the reasons below.

a.) Men don't do the shopping as much, and are therefore less inundated by the thousands of requests that make them more resistant to cards. Women in the US still do the majority of shopping, get the brunt of the requests, and have become used to automatically turning down credit card offers. Men also aren't as crazy about shopping, so Paco Underhill found that oftentimes men will say yes to customer offers just to get out of the store.

Also, I admit I am not above flirting in order to get men to open a credit card. (*Ooo, I just LOVE this color on men! Want to save 15% today?*) This is sexist and terrible and I apologize to Susan B. Antonio, but I have *gots* to hit my credit goals!

b.) Cards are a BIG American thing, and people from other countries are less wary, probably because they haven't been burned by overdraft fees yet. I also speak a smattering of Spanish, and my Spanish speakers think I am cute when I butcher their language, and often open credit cards up because they feel sorry for the poor American girl who is bumbling through their language like Andre the Giant in a yoga class. (*Quiere una tarjeta de credito? Gracias!*)

c.) I can talk the young people into credit cards because they don't know any better. They are new to the credit card world, wide-eyed baby bunnies suddenly discovering the joys of buying now and paying later.

Do I sound terrible? A con artist? I'm honestly not. I always carefully explain the benefits and the drawbacks, and I make them swear on their newly bought clothing that they will *pay off the balance in full each month*. I prefer if they have cash or check that they pay it off that very minute so they don't have a balance. I do not want anyone to go into debt or get a bad credit rating. The good thing about our card is that if they pay it off every month their credit rating will go up. Which leads to my next point–

2.) **Like Your Product**. It is really, really hard to sell something that you don't like. *So hey, do you want this credit card? It's great. Do I have it? Oh, no, I wouldn't open a card here.* Who is going to go for that? I'm a good seller because I like our credit card. I've had it since my second week at the store, and I can work the credit card coupons like RuPaul works the runway. People can sense your sincerity and will know if you are trying to sell them something worthless. So find out everything you can about your product and figure out a way to like it.

3.) **Be Cool.** People don't respond well to over-enthusiastic selling. Maybe we are all traumatized by high school, where caring too much meant you were a chronic dork, and the cool kids were the ones who were the most laid-back. Either way, people like when you are chill. *So, this card is really pretty great. I've had it for five years and it gets you discounts every month. I think you'd like it. But if not, that's cool.* People are less suspicious then when you are leaning across the counter towards them, frantically listing all the card benefits like a wild-eyed infomercial.

4.) **Learn to Calculate**. Little did I know that my bartending experience would contribute to my retail success. Mainly how now I can calculate tips faster than Isaac Newton with a T-9 calculator. This comes hugely in handy in the credit card world. People don't like percents, they like dollars. *I'll save 25% of $150? Ew, don't need it. But wait, you say I'll save almost 40 bucks? Now I'm interested.*

Learn my trick - base everything off 10%. Whatever the total is, drop the last digit.

185 dollars - drop the 5 - 10% is about $18
227 dollars - drop the 7 - 10% is about $22
88 dollars - drop the 8 - 10% is about $8

Easy enough, right? Now you can start manipulating. Is your store discount 20% today? Double your 10%.

18 bucks at 10%, 18+18 = 36
22 bucks at 10%, 22+22 = 44
8 bucks at 10%, 8+8 = 16

Ooo but wait - say it's 15%! No problem. Take HALF of your original 10% and ADD it to your original 10% again!

1/2 of 18 is 9, 18+9 = 27
1/2 of 22 is 11, 22+11=33
1/2 of 8 is 4, 8+4 = 12

Learn this trick. Don't use a calculator. It takes away precious moments that you could be using to brain-wash your customer.

Going along with the calculation trick....

5.) **Push the Big Purchases.** I have opened cards on purchases of a two-dollar Hallmark card, but for the easy wins, go for the big buys.

Like a predatory retail eagle I will scan overhead what's in the customer's cart, then as I scan I keep a running tally of what the percent off will be. A few items before the end I'll casually remark, "Do you have our card yet? If you don't, you'll save over $70 today." I round up to a nice fat number. Seeing a pair of athletic shoes or, the holy grail, a Dyson vacuum, makes me swoon against the counter. Dysons are usually 500 dollars, so at the least percent the customer will save 50 bucks, at the highest end - $150! That is usually a credit slam dunk.[5]

It is a good thing I am a good credit card salesperson, because credit rules our world. We get daily quotas that we have to hit, or else many bad things happen to us. Hours get cut, the DM calls and yells at us, our scorecard drops - it's a domino effect of sucking. I have spoken to many higher-ups, and though they are required to rave about the benefits, they all hate the card as much as the minions do.

---

[5] I'll watch my associates, and if they can't open a card on a $500 dollar purchase, it's a bad indication of their sales skills. No more POS for you, Billy!

There's so much pressure to open credit cards and hit goals that cheating runs rampant throughout all the country's stores. One associate got fired for making up Social Security numbers and opening fake cards to hit goals. The month before she had been featured in the company newsletter as one of the top credit producers in the country. Whoops. Other associates make members of their family open cards. I personally pressure the Associates to open cards. If I can't make customers open 'em, I can make my team open 'em.[6]

Other cheating methods include giving higher percents or more dollars off for opening a card. Corporate is very strict on this being a big no-no. I can't figure out why. They have total boners for credit but only want to give 10% off to the customer for opening a card. I live in Washington. 10% barely covers tax. Plus we have specials all the time for 25% off, 30% off,

---

[6] In my defense, they *work* at the store. They spend their *money* in the store. They might as well get the *coupons* from the store, right?

$10 off. Why not give them to customers to make our credit goals easier?[7]

The second worst job on the floor, after cashier (see Chapter 11), is the floor credit associate. They have to wander around the floor and harass customers while they are shopping. Trust me, these people are not open to opening a credit card from the random associate pestering them while they are looking at bra and panty sets. Awk-ward.

So Corporate loves credit cards and stupid projects, but what they hate is to close any store, at any time, for any reason. One year we had the snow day to end all snow days. I live in the Northwest where two inches can close down a school. This was a snow day consisting of a blinding, state-wide blizzard and a new record for inches of snow per hour. We had THIRTY-TWO people call out. I stopped answering the phone because it got too depressing. It was me and Jeanie, our sixty-year old shoe associate, running the 17-million-a-year store by ourselves. Which was not a problem because

---

[7] I don't have an answer for this. But thanks for visiting this footnote!

every customer in the Northwest was at home obeying the news reporter's insistence that they go home and not leave under any condition.

After countless phone calls from me, each one more desperate the last, when do you think Corporate agreed to let us close down the store two hours early?

Exactly. After the power went out.

Then, and only then, did Jeanie and I lock up the store, stumble out into the blizzard, and climb onto our sleds to mush our sled dogs home.

The reason I made Jeanie stick it out with me was the story I just heard about an ASM in California being fired. Apparently, it was seven PM on a Tuesday night and the store was dead. Little tumbleweeds were rolling by registers while sassy roadrunners made the loop around the sales race track. The ASM decided, hey, why not, let's save some payroll and close up shop!

So she did, and Corporate freaked out worse than Britney Spear's manager after she shaved her head. The woman couldn't have been fired faster if she had streaked naked through the Juniors department while smacking customers with sales flyers.

Corporate doesn't want to lose out on any dollars, you see. This also contributes to the insanity that is Black Friday. Retail companies keep rolling back opening on Black Friday until we opened on Thanksgiving itself (Thanksgiving 2014- open at 6 pm!). The trouble with that is many customers don't like it. They feel like big jerks making all of us work on a holiday.[8] When we only close for three holidays a year, it's pretty sad when one of them is taken away. If Corporate could feasibly do it I think we would all be 7-11s, open 24 hours a day, 365 days a year. That may be the track they're on. All I hope is either I'm long gone at that point, or we've created very sophisticated retail robots that can fold on demand and don't whine about getting enough hours. *That* is the project Corporate should have me work on.

And so we struggle on with Corporate demands, picking and choosing the projects we

---

[8] This is ironic, because they sure don't feel guilty starting their shopping at 10:50pm when we close at 11, thereby forcing us to stay later. Ah, well, I'll take the guilt where I can get it.

want to work on and cheating on credit cards along the way. Corporate's goal is to make big money. There are very few non-profit retailers out there. The best way they know how to make money is to squeeze us on the store end, since they don't feel the pain on their end. Corporate is not going to change. At least until the retail robots get invented.

Chapter 5
Returns, or Seriously? You're Really Returning This?

"Stupidity isn't punishable by death. If it was, there would be a hell of a population drop."
-Laurell K. Hamilton

Many stores have strict return policies. To prevent loss to the bottom line, the company executives create long, winding return policies, explaining exactly when, where, and how the purchased items can be returned. The policies are often outlined in tiny 1-point font on the back of receipts, looking like microscopic posters for mice optometry exams. 90 days exactly, repackaging fees, shipping fees, and you've washed it? Forget it!

I envy those stores' employees.

My store is not one of these stores. My store accepts anything. Absolutely everything. For your convenience, let me provide an exhaustive list of what our store will take back.

What We Accept in Returns

1.) Worn stuff

2.) Washed stuff

3.) Broken stuff

4.) Stuff that is missing key pieces, such as a grill without the actual grill

5.) Stuff that has obviously been stolen

6.) Stuff that customers say they bought a few weeks ago, but they actually bought it 45 years ago as gifts for their children, who are now receiving Social Security checks

7.) Stuff from other stores that customers insist they bought at our store, even if we explain that no, we do not carry the brand, "Old Navy." Old Navy generally carries the brand "Old Navy".

So to reiterate - we would accept your fifty year old, smelly, used, dirty clothing and your nasty, broken, mutilated housewares. You break it? We'll take it. Our store knows that customers are more likely to buy stuff if they can return it, and the more they buy, the more likely they'll keep it. It's a sound business model, except when you're on the receiving end of the returns.

You don't believe me on what we accept? Read the next few stories. These are all honest-to-God, true stories that happened in my store. The names have been changed to protect the crazy.

This Box Rocks

Last year, a sketchy customer came in with a huge cooking set that we sell for $300. He brought the receipt, and our Customer Service employee happily scanned it, took the box, gave him the money, and put the box in the go-back area. No problems, no concerns. I assume the associate was whistling some joyful song to himself.

Later that day, my other manager lifted up the box to take it out to the floor. It rattled, *loudly*. She cocked her head to the side, and asked the associate, "Why does this cookware seem so loose?"

He shrugged, smiling the smile of the truly carefree. And dumb.

She popped open the top and saw.....rocks. Piles and piles of grey rocks.

My store just paid 300 bucks. For rocks.

Mice Mice Baby

Often times customers bring in their plastic bags for returns, and drop them unceremoniously on my counter. I stare at the customer, and then I stare at the bag, long enough for the customer to become uncomfortable. If they don't take the hint, I pinch the corner of the bag with my thumb and forefinger, pulling the bag upwards in a slow, repulsed motion, until the item drops out of the bag and onto the counter. Customers may be annoyed with my obvious disgust, but ask me if I care.

I'll tell you if I care. No. I don't.

The reason for my repulsion is two years ago, my associate Clara was working the returns counter. A sleazy-looking couple dressed in ill-fitting shirts and holey jeans wandered up and placed a moldy, old plastic bag onto the counter.

"How can I help you folks today?" Claire said perkily.

"Return." The man mumbled, looking away from her. The woman fidgeted and glanced from the right and the left, rubbing her nose rapidly. We have learned in retail to peg drug dealers very quickly, and these two were big-time users. The man rocked on his heels twitchily and waited for Clara to pull out the item.

Clara willingly reached into the bag, and let out a shriek as a small streak of white furry lightening booked it out of the bag and launched itself off the counter. The people had a MOUSE in the bag! The mouse had obviously snuck into the nasty bag at the nasty people's home, and it was probably delighted to escape into a brand-new store to call its own.

We called the exterminators, and eventually the mouse was captured and summarily disposed of, after leading us on a great three-day mouse chase. I regretted it though. He was a brave little soul, escaping from his sty of a home and traveling to great lengths to make his new home at our shiny store. I admired the moxie of the little mouse.

I still won't reach into a customer's bag anymore, though.

I Ink, Therefore I Am

It was late on a Tuesday night, and we were getting ready to finish up our late-night recovery, when a woman lurched into our store and made her way drunkenly to my customer service counter. My associate Juliet and I glanced nervously at each other. She plunged her hand into a rival store's reusable bag, thrust around, and triumphantly pulled out a small, one inch by one inch black square and smacked it on our returns counter. I picked the tiny box up and examined it.

"What...is it?" I asked carefully.

"It's a baby hand-print kit," the drunken lady replied, leaning on the counter for support.

I glanced at Juliet, who shrugged at me. "I haven't seen us sell one of those." She told me under her breath.

"Oh, you sell it." Boozy said, her eyes glazed, holding onto the counter with both hands.

I scanned her receipt and the item. It popped up as $29.50. I glanced at the tiny ink pad again. It was about half the size of a coaster, and it certainly didn't look like it cost almost thirty dollars, unless the ink was made from rare octopus ink.

"Ma'am, did this come with anything else?" I asked her.

"No." she replied in a slurred voice, still holding onto the counter with all her strength in an attempt to keep upright.

"It didn't come with a box? An instruction kit? A book to actually put the handprints in?" I pressed her.

"Oh yes, I guess, maybe." She shrugged, bothered that I was asking her all of these *questions.* Her vodka was waiting for her back home!

So you can guess what I did. I told her, "Absolutely not, you boozehound. Out you go!"

HAH! What store do you think I work at?

OF COURSE I TOOK THE RETURN. I handed the money back to my alcoholic customer, who was no doubt going to use it to invest in her

401(k). But I was tough on her. "Next time, ma'am, when you do a return, we're going to ask you to return it with *all* the pieces."

Take *that.*

Zoya

Zoya, the Insane Return Queen, is a staple in our store. Zoya is a plump lady from Eastern Europe, with graying hair she tucks under a paisley scarf, and never less than five relatives in her wake. I'm sure every store has a Zoya. Since our store opened, she's been there. Arguing over our prices, trying to combine numerous non-combinable coupons at a time, and most importantly, returning totally inappropriate things. We all love Zoya, basically because she's certifiably insane. As far as I'm concerned, the week is a failure without a good Zoya story.

Zoya takes a prime role in the next few return stories.

Transitions

When Zoya had her baby (number seven, I think), she bought two little pink newborn jumpers, one with a cat, one with a sheep. The jumpers were a basic style that we had in stock for the last few years, in all children's sizes, with white lace around the ankles and Peter Pan collars.

Three months later, she exchanged the same (well-used) newborn pink jumpers for 3-6 month jumpers.

Six months after that for the 6-12 month sizes.

Six months later, she exchanged the *exact same jumpers* for toddler sizes!

We are lucky Osh Kosh B'Gosh does not make juniors clothing, or Zoya's daughter would have been wearing that pink sheep-ed jumper through puberty.

Sing It Loud, Sing It Proud

Twenty minutes before we closed on Fourth of July in 2011, Zoya returned forty patriotic t-shirts. Which went clearance the next day.

Which had the names of each person in her church choir group, written in puffy paint on the back.

Of. Every. Single. Shirt.

So we had forty patriotic T-shirts in our inventory that had to be sent back as a loss. Unless we had any customers who wanted to buy untimely holiday t-shirts with Boris, Ekaterina, or Yury written on them. Surprisingly, demand was not high for those that year.

What's The Problem Here?

My favorite Zoya story took place when I'd just gotten to my store. I was working the customer service desk and was training with Antonio, a fabulous gay man whose favorite task in the store was colorizing the men's ties.

Zoya marched up to the service desk, with approximately five rug rats tussling with each other behind her. Antonio looked at her and then looked at me, pity in his eyes. He took an infinitesimal step backward, leaving me in the direct line of fire of the aging European woman.

"I want to make return," Zoya stated firmly.

"No problem!" I said, cheerfully. "That's what we do!" Oh, how charming I was. I snuck a glance at Antonio, who was carefully pretending to be re-ticketing a pair of jeans while watching the exchange. I smirked at him. This was going to be easy. He smirked back. He knew better.

She took out her receipt and pointed at an item. "I want return this." It was a basic brand-name sweater, priced at $15.99.

"No problem," I said again, taking the receipt and scan the bar code on the computer. I held the scanner out, ready to scan her item to return. "So, where's the sweater?"

"I no have," she said.

What? I thought maybe I misheard her. "Sorry, ma'am. Where's the sweater?"

"I NO HAVE!" She said loudly, irritated at my stupidity. "I not going home to get. I get later. I need the money now." She stared me down across the counter. Her many kids fought with each other behind her, squabbling like little pigeons and pushing each other into the walls.

Timidly, I said, "Um, we generally have to get the item back to do a return." I offered a wimpy smile.

Antonio had turned his back to us, his back vibrating from silent laughter. I glared hate rays at him. Zoya didn't back down. She stared at me, daring me to refuse her. The kids moved on to squirting each other with the water fountain.

"Well, ma'am, how about... when you go get the sweater, we do the return then?" I asked, timorously. I kicked Antonio in the foot, and he turned back to me with a look of surprised innocence. My eyes told him exactly what I was going to do to him if he did not help me out.

Zoya glared at both of us, " You do return! I want money back! Or I want manager! I know return policy. Says you HAVE to do return!" One of the kids chimed in. "Yeah! HAVE to do return!" Zoya was training the future generation of Zoyas. God help us all.

Antonio smiled at me, and spoke to her in a soothing tone, "Now, Zoya, you know it's store policy to receive the item when you return something. Macy is a manager and she's just following the rules." He knew who she was! Jerkface.

Zoya gave us the Look of Death, grabbed her receipt, and turned on her heel. "I be back!" she yelled at us over her shoulder, herding the five Children of the Corn toward the door.

Antonio slapped me on the shoulder, "Welcome to retail, girlie."

Terrific.

After those first months of Zoya returns, I learned something important. The customer is not always right.

I am always right.

Another joy I have found in in retail is the expression on people's faces when I am proven correct on returns.

Sample conversation:

Customer: I know I bought that just a month or so ago!
Me: Oh, really? You didn't buy it in... (consulting my computer) ...hmmm, 2001? Because that's the last time we sold it.
Customer: ... *Silence*

Screw a Snickers bar. Now THAT is satisfaction.

Returns are a fact of life in retail. As a consumer, I love stores that have generous return policies. It's very annoying to have a 15-day only, un-opened, un-worn, un-used, can't-have-looked-at-the-item-too-hard return policy. People are tactile shoppers, and they need to try stuff on in the real world to see what works. I completely get that.

But as a retail employee, I hate generous return policies. Every return is more work for me. To all those of you who return your well-worn shoes, your cat-hair covered bedding, your disgusting, ten-year-old yellowing t-shirts - please keep in mind all those people at the stores have to deal with your gross stuff. Think about whether you should really return an item before you do it. Ask yourself, "Is this the manufacturer's fault, or did I misuse it?" If you are really going to return it, be polite and respectful at the counter, and pretty please, *bag up your used underwear.* Handling that is straight-up grossbuckets.

Also, since our return policy is so liberal, I don't need to hear your dramatic retelling of the saga of the purchased item. Most people feel the need to enlighten me on exactly why they're returning it. "So I bought this tank top last week and I wore it to my daughter's cheerleading practice because they are practicing for state and I got home and saw that it was fraying just a bit on the strap but I didn't worry about it because it was tiny but then the next day I saw it was a little bigger and I decide to sew it but I didn't have the right color thread and I also saw a small tear at the seam and so I thought I'd bring it in can I return it?" Meanwhile, I have already scanned, returned, and retagged the item five seconds into this little speech. I tell the customer, "No problem. NEXT!" Then the next person comes up and says, "So I bought this pair of shoes yesterday and we went on a boat ride around the lake on my friend's new sailboat and I saw a small stain on the insole..."

We accept EVERYTHING. I don't CARE why you're returning this. I care why you're still in my line keeping me from my break. Move along, cowpoke.

And finally, to end the returns chapter, here is a Returns Public Service Announcement: Please do not return anything if you see me working the customer service desk. Thank you.

Especially if your name is Zoya.

Chapter 6

The Bad, Bad, Bad, Bad Boss

"Bosses are like legs. When they get to the top, they become asses."

-Unknown

I hated my first boss in retail.

Like, serious hatred. Working for him I found he was a selfish, spoiled, inconsiderate, power-driven, patronizing, condescending, arrogant, ignorant, self-satisfied, smug, repulsive little slug-faced piece of worm poo.

Most times, when a person hates his or her boss, the problem usually lies within. If you hate every person you've ever worked for, chances are pretty high that YOU are the problem, not management. But I hold myself exempt from this, because I have had ten managers in the duration of my career and I have adored them all. Until the worm poo came along.

This boss made retail hell. Fine, calling retail hell is repetitious, but he truly did.

I am a very obedient employee. Years of school have created in me the Good-Student Syndrome, in which I listen patiently, raise my hand when I need to speak, and take the word of all authority figures to be law. Not only do I have Good-Student Syndrome, I have the Daddy-Boss Complex, where I see my boss as my father and am always scared that I'm going to get grounded when I'm in trouble. This all works just fine when you have an excellent boss who makes good decisions, but it is a real problem when your boss is incompetent.

According to CNBC there are 5 **Types** of bad bosses.

1. The Bully. The bully makes a toxic workplace, publicly or privately threatening and humiliating employees.

2. The Micromanager. The micromanager keeps a tight leash, helicoptering over employees' shoulders to manage every little detail.

3. The Poor Communicator. It's important to give employees space and not

micromanage, but it's crucial to give them enough direction to get the job done. The poor communicator provides little direction, which often results in the tasks having to be completed — or even redone — at the last minute.

4. The Saboteur. He undermines the efforts of others. He doesn't give credit for a job well done — or worse, takes the credit himself. Then, he lays the blame on thick when things go wrong.

5. The Fickle Boss. This boss may be nice and all, but if she lacks clarity and decisiveness, it can leave employees confused and unproductive. Fickle boss can also have unpredictable mood swings — confiding in someone one day and turning on them the next.

My boss was, at one time or another, ALL FIVE of these bad boss types. This is pretty impressive when you consider the Micromanager and the Poor Communicator are the exact opposite of each other.

Then, there are the 5 **Traits** of bad bosses.

1. Arrogant. Bad bosses put themselves above the team and give themselves all the credit for success.

2. Opaque. It's not a new idea that transparency in management can instill trust and enables an organization to run better, since knowing what's going on helps people do their jobs. But that wisdom hasn't trickled down to many bad bosses.

3. Taciturn. Similarly, bad bosses minimize any type of problem, and don't share information about threats with the team, leaving them completely unprepared.

4. Undisciplined. Bad bosses have poor delegation skills and they don't manage the team.

5. Detached. A good boss truly cares about employees. Employees can tell if a boss isn't interested in them or their career development.

Again, impressively, my boss exhibited all five of these traits. He was a caricature of Dilbert's pointy-haired boss: demanding, conceited, misleading, uncommunicative, unresponsive, and in turns both a micromanager and too hands-off.

My first inkling that my boss was not up to par was during the first week I worked for him. But let me give you some background on how I was made to work for him in the first place.

When I first began in retail, my eyes bright and my tail bushy, my district manager decided to put me, after careful consideration, where he thought I would learn the most – the worst store in the country. This is a true story. I had just finished the manager training program and I was a bench manager, which meant I didn't come out of the DM budget. Thus, he thought he'd save some money and stick me in the store that was ranked dead-last: number 1159 out of 1159 stores. And believe me, I learned a lot. Mainly, what not to do.

The freedom of being in the worst store in the country is that you can't possibly make it worse. My jewelry supervisor had called out fifty-two times in the last year. This is not an exaggeration. She had called out the equivalent of over *two solid months* of business days. Most stores have less than a hundred pieces of backstock clearance. We had 30,000 pieces of clearance in the back stockroom that we couldn't figure how to get to the floor. The average number of shoe mismates is about five to seven single shoes in any store. We had *a hundred and forty* - and that was just the ones in the back, never mind the chaos of mismatched, incorrectly sized shoes on the floor!

The 30,000 pieces of clearance in the back was my favorite. We had clearance from the early 90s. The awesomeness of that was the items had missed about forty rounds of clearance markdowns, so everything was like 99% off. I bought a full-length gold mirror for a $2.49, a three-piece suit for my husband for $14, and basically everything in my kitchen for less than 20 bucks.

To illustrate the standard of our store recovery (recovery is the code word for cleaning up the store), let me give you an example. One time my coworker stuck a pink kid's T-shirt in the middle of the women's swimwear rack. We took bets on when our associates would notice it and/or put it back where it belonged. Every day one of us would check on the shirt, and every day it remained stuck conspicuously in the middle of women's bikinis. *Three months later* we saw it had been put away. Not by our associates. Oh no. By the *janitor,* who had picked it up after he had seen it fall on the floor! It had missed clearance markdowns six times over. This was the standard of our floor recovery. As you can imagine, our store was a big hit with customers.

This was where the terrible boss ruled.

Bad Bad Boss was the reason this store was a failure, for all the bad boss reasons listed above. He was so arrogant that he knew the best way to do everything; he listened to no one. He hid his badness well during my first day, but on my second day on the job Bad Boss pulled me into his office.

"Macy," he said. "What is the most important path to success in retail?"

Eager to please, I said, "Customer service!" I beamed, confident that customers were the end-all-be-all of a store.

"Ah," he said, lifting a finger. "No. Sales."

I stared at him. "But..." I said, "Don't you need customers for sales?"

He laughed patronizingly. "Yes, they can be important. But sales are the most important thing. They mean everything to the higher-ups."

He leaned towards me. "I've been in retail for fifteen years. Trust me, I know a few things about sales. And I'll teach you what you need to know."

Forcing a smile, I nodded, not so sure about working for this guy. Over the next few months, this is what he taught me:

- Don't schedule enough people during closing shifts to save payroll. You can always frantically call associates at 4 PM on a Saturday night and try to talk them into coming in. Associates love canceling weekend plans to come clean up the store.

- Spend the majority of your payroll during the first two weeks, then spend the last two weeks desperately cutting much-needed projects. Be sure not to learn your lesson so you do it again the next month.

- Definitely don't schedule enough people for major projects. People are always willing to stay past their ten-hour shift to finish a poorly planned project when they are exhausted.

• Talk down to everyone below you. This shows how important you are and how you know better than everybody, which equates into respect.

• Take a really long time to explain something simple, and then gloss over the definition of something difficult. This shows you care enough to explain, but that you are far too busy to explain anything complex.

• Never hold employees accountable. You can always make your good employees work harder to make up for the slacking of your bad employees.

• If you do have to hold someone accountable, make sure your associate managers do it for you. That way, if an employee sues the company, you are in the free and clear.

• If you are angry when an employee calls out, be sure to hang up on them. This shows your irritation, and they will be much more likely to want to come in for their next shift.

• Never fire anyone, even if they deserve it. This looks bad on your turnover report. It's much better to keep bad employees on the payroll until they quit the day before Black Friday, screwing your entire team and your sales plan.

• The best way to scold an associate is to do it in public. Public shaming is the most effective.

Let me give you a quick example of this one. One morning before our AM meeting, my boss noticed someone had written on our store news whiteboard, "Our Store Sucks." Not mature, I grant you, but we employed a lot of high school students, and truthfully, our store did suck. But the boss was *furious.* Like, Incredible Hulk furious. He grabbed the nearest overhead pager and called a store-wide meeting on the very spot. "All employees are to come to the stockroom at once. **NOW!!**"

When everyone had gathered, he pointed to the blue-scribbled message.

"Who wrote this?" he demanded. People fidgeted, not making eye contact.

"Who wrote this??" he said, louder. No one came forward. The boss sucked in his breath.

"Now listen to me." he said, quietly and menacingly. "There are cameras in every corner of this store. I mean, every single corner. I am going to go watch the videos with Loss Prevention, and I assure you, I will find out who did this. If you come to me now and admit it, it will be better for you." He sounded like a medieval Inquisitor. *Admit ye wrongdoing and ye shall be spared!* The group looked uncomfortable and time passed in a slow march. Finally, our juniors specialist, a tiny blonde with bright red acne and an unfortunate potbelly took a step forward. "It was me." She admitted in a low voice.

"Thank you, Sapphire, for being honest." My boss said. She gave a small smile, showing her gapped teeth. "You're fired." He added.

Everyone murmured in shock. Sapphire looked aghast. "I thought....I thought if I admitted it you'd go easy on me."

The boss smiled. "Maybe next time you won't insult the company you work for." He said. "Pack your locker up. I'm calling LP to have you escorted out." Everyone muttered in anger at the double-cross. I felt my stomach turn and churn at the discomfort of the situation.

Sapphire headed to the breakroom to pack up her stuff in a fury. People began dispersing back into the store, still upset. "Oh, and by the way, Sapphire," my boss called over his shoulder. "There are no cameras in the stockroom." She whipped around in shock. He grinned at her and gave her a cocky little goodbye wave.

So this was the caliber of man I was working for.

Two months into my servitude under Bad Boss's regime, we had a visit from the Vice President of stores and the Vice President of the entire retail company. This is the equivalent of the Speaker of the House and the Vice President of the United States, in retail perspective. The bad boss was in full-on panic mode, flitting around the store like a hummingbird on uppers. I was in charge of managing the front end and keeping the fitting rooms clean, a daunting job on the best of days. To top it off we had a truck that day, which meant our associates were balancing floor duties with putting out freight, which they were not so good at.[9]

I was hitting all the fitting rooms in a frantic clean-up cycle, unsure where the managers were on their walk. I checked Boys-Girls-Men's-Juniors-Misses, repeat. The walks would generally start in the front and work their way to the dock, then finish up in the office. After two hours of incessant loops, they were nowhere to be found, and my hands began to unclench a little while my shoulders dropped with a slight sense of respite. Then out of nowhere, the walkie crackled to life, and the sputtering sound dropped a cannonball of fear into the depths of my stomach.

"Macy?" My boss asked in a controlled voice. "Get someone into the women's fitting room. *Now.*"

Calculating, I tried to remember how long it had been since I'd been there. I raced across

---

[9] Fine, they weren't that good at anything. You caught me.

the store, barreling past confused customers. The walkie crackled again.

"Macy?" My boss said. "Don't worry about it. The vice-president of the company is cleaning it out."

Yes. Our VP was cleaning out our fitting room. This was the retail equivalent of Joe Biden cleaning the White House restrooms.

Needless to say, the walk was a total success. Not. This was the same walk where the VP of stores pulled me aside and said, in a measured tone, "You're a manager-in-training? All right then. Let me train you. Everything you learned in this store = Do. Not. Do."

The end of the terrible boss came two days before Christmas, the busiest sales time of the year, when our Human Resources ASM and the administrative assistant (who had been having an affair) both walked out on us. They then called the District Manager, the Human Resources Director for the West Coast, and the Vice President of Territories 1-4 to tattle on everything the boss had been up to for the last year. The District Manager called the Bad Bad Boss and told him that in case he was thinking about showing up to work the next day, he might want to reconsider. That was the last I saw of the 5-B Boss.

In case you were wondering about the terrible store, after another six months of retail decadence and two-dollar clearance, my District Manager decided to get serious and put a new store manager who actually knew what he was doing in the store to clean it up. It took him over two solid years to get the store back into acceptable condition.

I wasn't there during the renovation, because I had transferred to a different state to be near my husband (my fiancée at the time). Funnily enough, the next store I was transferred to turned out to be the number one store in the company. It was a pretty big and unintentional coincidence to go from Store #1159 out of 1159 stores to #1 out 1159 stores. Stores are ranked by a giant scorecard, including sales, customer service surveys, associate surveys, recovery standards, and credit card sales. This means the rankings can fluctuate, but this store stayed number one or two off and on for years. (Terrible store stayed consistently the worst. One April we jumped up to Store number 1025 in the company instead of 1159 out of 1159. We had a celebratory pizza party.)

Imagine my surprise when I found myself working in a store with actual standards. And accountability! Whoa. People watched what I did and told me if it was correct or not! Too weird. I learned things I never learned before - like that it was actually *not* acceptable to change prices for associates, honor a dollar-off coupon multiple times, or accept returns from other retailers. Surprise!

Now follow me closely here. Worst store in the company = worst boss. Best store in the company = best boss.[10] I could have worked for my best boss for my entire life and been happy. Bad bosses not only affect your happiness, they can affect your health. In a Swedish study, 3,000 employed men between 18 and 70 years of age were tracked for almost a decade. They examined the number of fatal and non-fatal heart disease occurrences. They found a 25% greater risk for employees with the least competent managers. If the person had had been

---

[10] I got an MBA. Partly because of my keen deductive reasoning skills.

with the bad boss for four years or more, there was a *64% greater heart disease risk*!

So if you joke about your boss being so bad he's killing you - he may be actually killing you! If you've ever thought about becoming self-employed - now just may be the time. Or you could always come work for me. I am a Good Good Good Good Good Boss.

My husband thinks so, anyway.

Chapter 7

Fitting Rooms and Recovery, or, Did Your Mama Raise You Like That?!

"It is more comfortable for me, in the long run, to be rude than polite."

-Wyndham Lewis

It was a glorious day for me, the day that will live on forever. It was May 19, 2014. The sun was shining, summer was coming to the

Northwest, and joy was in the air. It was that day, that beautiful day.... the day I guilted a customer into hanging her clothes back up and bringing them out of the fitting room.

Oh, I had tried before. Six years of trying, to be precise. I would come into fitting rooms with piles of clothes up to my waist. Clothes tangled with piles of jewelry, crammed into inside-out khakis. I would say loudly to the exiting woman, "Are you all done in there?" staring pointedly at Mount Rejects. I always got one of three replies:

1.) "Yes, thank you!" with a big, toothy grin. This means, "That's your job. YOU clean it."

2.) A vacant look and half-smile in my direction as the customer wanders out. This means, "I really, truly have no idea that I just left forty-five minutes of work on the floor."

3.) Heads down, abashedly looking at the floor, no comment and a guilty scurry out through the door. What this means is, "I feel deeply guilty, but there is NO WAY I am hanging up those dresses."

I glanced under the fitting room doors to scope out the situation, and I saw a pile of clothes willy-nilly on the floor of the far right fitting room. A small blonde woman on a cell phone swung open the door, and sashayed down the aisle. I stopped her on her way and did my usual spiel. I interrupted her conversation and said, extra-cheerily, "Are you all finished in that room? Nothing left?" She stopped mid-sentence, halting her chitchat, and looked at me. And, amazingly, she turned on her heel and went back in. I was astonished. She spent several minutes in there, and lo and behold, brought out her clothes, *hung correctly,* to the fitting room bar.

The refrain from Hallelujah Chorus resounded throughout my head.

What was it that actually worked this time? Was it the combined guilt of the person on the phone being a presence? How can I patent this?

Needless to say, it has never - not ever - worked again.

Fitting rooms are a battleground where an unending struggle commences every day. People take clothes into fitting rooms, try stuff on, decide they don't want it, and leave it for the retail associates to put away. I don't know how this practice got started but I am opposed.

Forgive me for the next paragraph. This is truly a rant. I cannot believe people who take fifty items into the fitting room and leave them on the floor. What does your house look like? Did your mama really raise you like that? The kids in fitting rooms we can forgive. Teenagers, maybe. But full-grown men and women– how can you justify making a big mess and leaving it for someone else to clean up? Sure, they'll say it's our job. That we get paid for doing it. But let me tell you – every minute we don't have to spend cleaning up after you, we could spend restocking the shelves so you can find what you want. We could spend that minute learning the answers to your questions about an item. We could spend that time ringing you up at the register, getting you out of the store quickly.

But no. Instead, I will spend that time scooping up inside-out capris off the floor and hanging countless sundresses. And I will hate you for it.

I saw a sign in a small retail store that should be immediately installed in all fitting rooms, all retailers, nationwide.

You. You reading this book.

Take the following test.

Am I a Dressing Room Douchebag?

A True or False Quiz

1.) You take 15 pairs of identical blue jeans into the fitting room. After trying on two pairs, you decide you dislike the color and leave the rest in a pile on the floor.

2.) You try on underwear frequently. And not over the pair you're wearing.

3.) You don't want to go into a fitting room, so you take your shirt off by the nearest mirrored pillar and let everyone enjoy your shopping process.

4.) You think to yourself, "Well, they'll just have to rehang it anyway, so I may as well not hang it." You then leave a mountain of tangled spaghetti strap tops in a giant ball on the fitting room chair.

5.) You ask an employee to find you the small, medium, and large size of the shirt you are wearing in pink, blue, green, chartreuse, maroon, and black. You try on each and every one of these. You then decide the style doesn't suit you and buy nothing.

6.) You bring your mother, best friend, sister, and miscellaneous cousins with you into the fitting room and cram yourselves into the largest stall, each person carrying twenty items each.

7.) You shout commands over the stall door at your hapless fitting room employee, making them search for things in your own personal store-wide scavenger hunt from hell and pulling them away from their fitting room duties for hours. Then, as they collapse exhausted by the fitting room cart, you breeze out the door with a single clearance tank top and a cheery thanks.

8.) You leave any one of the following things in the fitting room: empty coffee container, sticky soda can, crumpled candy bar wrapper, apple core, gum stuck to the wall, ground goldfish crackers in the carpet, or fast food remnants. Extra Credit Point: Tampon. Extra Extra Credit: Used Tampon.

9.) For some reason, you subconsciously decide the workers in the store need some fun, so you cram clothes underneath benches, over the fitting room doors, or in any nook and cranny to provide them with a riveting game of Hide and Go Seek Merchandise.

10.) You have left a fitting room looking like this:

If you answered True:

For 1-3 questions: You have douchebag tendencies.

For 4-6: You are on a precarious path to douchebaggery but can still resist, providing you start hanging up your fitting room outfits today.

For 7-9 questions: You will need a douchebag intervention soon for self-preservation before a retail employee strangles you to death with your own tried-on pants.

For 10 questions: Do not shop anymore. Anywhere. Ever.

The other half of our lives that we don't spend cleaning fitting rooms, we spend cleaning the store. Recovery is a general retail term, meant to cover up the actual sucky meaning of the word. It's similar to calling slaughtered baby lambs veal.

Recovery means clean up. It means folding shirts, sorting clothing on racks, picking up stuff off of the floor, throwing away dumped garbage, and leaving the store presentable so that the next day customers can traipse in and mess it all up again. It is a tireless, unending job, and I have spent countless hours trying to analyze it while stuffing ripped-out pajamas back into boxes.

I've always propagated the Broken Window Theory for recovery in retail. The Broken Window Theory stems from studies done by Philip Zimbardo, a Stanford psychologist, reported in 1969 and further clarified by two social scientists in an article titled "Broken Windows" which appeared in a 1982 Atlantic Monthly. Zimbardo arranged to have an automobile without license plates parked with its hood up on a street in the Bronx. He also placed a similar automobile vehicle, locked and properly parked, on a street in Palo Alto, California.

The car in the Bronx was attacked by "vandals" within ten minutes of its "abandonment." The first to arrive were a family -- father, mother, and young son -- who removed the radiator and battery. Within twenty-four hours, virtually everything of value had been removed. Then random destruction began -- windows were smashed, parts torn off, the upholstery ripped. Children began to use the car as a playground. So it's just what you would've expected, right? Rough neighborhood leads to vandalism. Duh. But a nice neighborhood- now the car will be fine and dandy.

The car in Palo Alto *did* sit untouched for more than a week. But then Zimbardo smashed part of it with a sledgehammer. Soon afterwards, passers-by were joining in. Within a few hours, after sitting unmolested for a week, the car had been turned upside down and utterly destroyed. People had seen that the car was getting destroyed and jumped in to help it along.

What happened was both in the rough neighborhood and the nice neighborhood, the cars were vandalized only after it was clear something was amiss. In the rough neighborhood it was the hood up, in the nice neighborhood it was the smashed windows. People steered clear of the cars until the mental barrier was removed - mainly, someone else had already started the destruction.

The usual example given is the broken window in a building, hence the title of the theory. If the window is not fixed as soon as possible, the bad elements (whatever that is for that neighborhood) surmise that no one cares, so they smash the remaining windows. Conversely, if it is fixed immediately, the bad element knows that people are aware and active in the neighborhood and don't mess with it. The theory's famous success story happened when New York Mayor Rudy Giuliani and NYPD chief William Bratton cleaned up New York's crime in the late 1990s. This involved cracking down on relatively small offenses such as graffiti, turnstile jumping, and the famous squeegeemen who would wash people's car windows without their request and then demand money. New York crime dropped substantially in the following years. The theory held that when you pay attention to the small problems, such as the squeegees,[11] they don't get a chance to turn into big problems.

This makes SO MUCH SENSE when you are folding down tables! The minute you see an unfolded shirt, you must pounce! Otherwise the customers see the unfolded shirt, assume that no one cares, and the unfolded shirts multiply like naughty bunnies. Most days I feel like Captain Kirk in a pile of Tribbles.[12]

An example of this is when a pair of underwear falls from its hanger. The customer

---

[11] I love the word squeegee. Squeegee squeegee squeegee squeegee squeegee squeegee. Okay, I'm done now.

[12] Because you need a Tribble picture.

immediately thinks, "Oh, other things are already on the ground. Other people have already knocked stuff down. Now I can do it too!"

After fifty customers think this, your store floor looks like this:

I would like to invite Rudy Giuliani and Bill Bratton to enforce their cleanup at my store. They would have the added bonus of being able to arrest people who made a mess, like stopping the squeegeemen in their tracks.[13] Which would be a dream come true.

So the Broken Window theory was always my theory in recovery. If we could keep the store immaculate, it would stay that way much longer because customers a.) would realize people cared and were looking out for them, and b.) wouldn't want to be the first ones to mess it up.

I believe this theory could hold true overall, but there is one theory–destroying, extremely-discouraging fact: people are slobs. None of my psych theories need to be applied to the piglets who shop in stores. They just feel entitled every day to bask in the thought, *"Someone else will clean up after me."*

Whenever I do recovery, I am reminded of those small coastal villages who, after being destroyed by a tsunami, patiently and carefully rebuild their town from scratch, only to have it destroyed again the following year.

People are tactile. They need to try stuff on. They need to feel the material, imagine how it

---

[13] Squeegee!

looks and will feel when they wear it. I totally get this. I am the same way. However, I still curse human nature whenever I walk into the Accessories department and see flip-flops scattered as far as the eye can see, like a perverted lily pond. I expect Kermit to start hopping from pair to pair. Try 'em on, sure. But why would you leave them all over the floor afterwards, Miss Piggy?

Same for rugs. People adore spreading rugs out to imagine how they will look in their living rooms. This is understandable. But when you are done - RE-FOLD THEM and PUT THEM AWAY! Why would you leave unfolded rugs all over the aisleway? Do you think people want to see your messy carpet collage?

Recovery is an endless battle that continues on throughout the ages. I feel certain that in the 1800s, the English haberdasher employees were complaining about messy 1800s customers. "I do say, that chap was a right slob. He left my ribbon piles all in a dither! That makes me so full peevish, I've 'alf a mind to collect some scuttlebutt and pen me a novel about it!"

Locked and Loaded

One time, I was amazed to find one of my associates completely ahead of the game on her fitting rooms. At that time of the night, normally our Misses associate would be slammed. I asked, "Mandy, how are you keeping up? What's your secret?"

Unabashed, Mandy pointed to the bay of fitting rooms. "I locked the last six fitting rooms so customers can't use them."

I choked and snorted, taken aback. "Mandy, you can't DO that!"

"Why not?" she asked. "Now customers can't mess them up!" It was ideal associate logic. Lock all the fitting rooms so no one could use them! I scolded her and made her open them again - but really, not such a bad idea. Our store would run so efficiently and look so beautiful if it wasn't for those stupid, messy customers!

Pick Up Your Shoes. Now.

Apparently, in some other countries, it's store policy that customers pick up after themselves. I want to live in these countries.

I learned this from Alexei, one of my shoe employees who was originally from Russia. How I learned this was listening to numerous customer complaints involving Alexei. Apparently, he would go up to customers and yell at them to clean up after themselves. Straight-up, he would order adults to pick their shoes up off of the floor, put them correctly in their boxes, and put them back on the shelves.

One customer told me that Alexei chased after him, kicking shoeboxes aside, and blocked him from leaving. Alexei shouted, "You leave giant mess! Go clean up!" The customer put his hands up, and tried backing away. Alexi advanced upon him, waving his arms. "Clean up your mess!" Alexei shouted maniacally.

It was very difficult to scold Alexei when he was doing what I dream of doing every single day.

All retail employees have fantasies on how they're going to leave when they finally quit. We all dream of doing a Steven Slater. Slater is the JetBlue flight attendant who cursed out all the customers onboard on the overhead speaker, grabbed a couple of beers, and shot down the emergency slide. To everyone in the customer service industry, Slater is a god and a hero.

My dream is to pull a Slater. Here is my how-I'm-going-to-quit fantasy:

It is Saturday afternoon. The stores is packed with shoppers: families with trailing children, old couples cruising the clearance racks, teen punks trying on flannel shirts and low rise jeans. I see my nemesis– the Hurricane Family. You can guess why I call them that. Hurricane Family has five, count 'em, five kids, ranging from 10 months to 7 years old.

The Hurricane Family is here for back-to-school shopping, and they are going to stock up. They start in the Girl's section, decimating the girl's underwear section as they methodically rip open the packages to examine the make. The mom decides the underwear won't do, and tosses the open packages on top of the fixtures. They move onto socks, making the kids try them on. After they are tried on, they are chucked back on the rack while they select a nice, new, un-tried-on pair of socks to actually purchase. Gross, who would buy a worn pair of socks? Certainly not the Hurricanes! No, they *mess the things up*, they don't *buy* them. That would be silly!

They select armfuls of clothing for all the kids, close to fifty items, and herd the troops into the fitting rooms, taking up all the stalls. The kids squeal and squawk at each other while the parents pull clothing over their heads.

They continue this trying-on process for an hour, accumulating a layer of clothes on the floor like an Alaskan snowfall. Victory achieved, they leave the destroyed fitting rooms and head to the registers, satisfied with all they have accomplished.

But not so fast.

This is my moment.

I stand before them in the aisle, hands on my hips, blocking their way. "Where do you think you're going?" I inquire coldly.

Mrs. Hurricane grins, clueless. "We are going to check out!" she exclaims. The children chatter behind her like enthusiastic bluejays. Her broad smile slips from her face when she sees my thunderous expression.

"No, you're not." I say, in a calm but irate tone. "You are going to turn around and clean up the mess you made." I point to the fitting room.

Mr. Hurricane looks aghast. "What? You don't have the right to..."

I cut him off. "I am not cleaning up your mess today." I say flatly.

The family stares at each other, wide-eyed. They've never been spoken to like this, even after all the stores they have destroyed. People nearby, customers and associates, perk their heads up and listen with interest.

"Go back to the fitting room. Hang everything up. Then go through all the packages you tore up and fix them. Do it, and do it **NOW!**" I bellow this last word, stepping towards them threateningly. The family stares at the insane employee, horrified.

Mr. Hurricane tries to stammer about poor treatment, and I make a fist and shake it at them. The atmosphere around us is charged as other people gather around to watch the show.

"This is unacceptable!" Mrs. Hurricane bellows, finding her voice. "You can't talk to us like that!"

"Today I can!" I say loudly. "Today I stand up for all retail workers who pick up after you every single time you come in. Now, get back into that fitting room and *CLEAN IT OUT!*" I point again in the direction of the fitting room. I glare at them with all the fury I can muster and the kids shrink behind their parents. I am the avenging retail angel. I am a superhero. I am ROAR - the Rant of a Retailer lion!

The Hurricanes scurry away like frightened cockroaches, dropping their items along the way. They weave towards customer service to find a manager to complain to, while the other patrons watch them go, then turn and look at me in fear.

Do I care? No. The nearby customers look aghast, but I know they are thinking twice about leaving their fitting rooms a mess. The employees clap and cheer me on as I take a bow and skip joyfully out the doors, unemployed. If I could take two beers and slide down the emergency slide, I would!

This fantasy runs through my head every time I see an annihilated rack or a tossed-upon fitting room chair. This is how I'm going out of retail.

And it's going to be so worth it.

Chapter 8

Things That Annoy Me: A Condensed List

"I like long walks, especially when they are taken by people who annoy me."
-Noel Coward

As you can tell if you have read this far, I simply hate to complain.[14] However, in those very rare, few and far-between instances that I have been irritated in my store, I find the best way to let go is to write it down. And then publish it in a snarky retail book.

Here is a very short list of all the things that annoy me in my store. If you would like the extended version, all you have to do is take me to Happy Hour and feed me key-lime martinis. I can promise you a good non-stop three hours of

---

[14] Hah!

the extended list, especially after a shift working during the full moon.[15]

Things That Annoy Me:

Associates who think I know everything in the store. This is flattering, but they will page me and ask, "Hey, where did the twelve-pack of steak knives get moved to?" I am not a personal inventory system. We have close to half a million items in the store. As brilliant as I am, I cannot keep track of every item we sell.

People who bring things up to the register they don't intend to buy. I can understand not purchasing an item at the register because you didn't know the price, but on a daily basis I have customers who plop their pile of clothes in front of me and start a sorting game. "I'll take this...I won't take this....I'll get this....no, I don't want that...." Half the pile ends up in a big messy go-back lump that I have to put away after. I had a customer bring up EIGHT rugs to the register and decide against buying ANY of them. Could you not have decided on the

---

[15] Fact - crazy people do come out more during full moons, but it's not a werewolf thing. They simply have more light to do their craziness by.

large and heavy rugs BEFORE you brought them all the way up to the register?

Breastfeeding in very obvious public. One afternoon, minding my own business, I was accosted by a giant white boob. The woman was breast-feeding her child in the front entryway with her shirt pulled down on the left side down to her navel. I'm all for breast-feeding, but dang. I get plenty of naked breasts in the intimates fitting room. This is another reason why I plan on leaving retail someday. I don't see any investment bankers having this kind of problem. If they do, it's probably at night and they probably pay for it.

Customers who blame associates when obviously it is so not our fault. Recently, I walked behind the customer service counter and a woman pounced. "Are you the manager?" She demanded to know. "Yes I am." I said, preparing myself for the onslaught. "YOU are the one who said we couldn't have the display!" She shrieked. "Actually ma'am, it's a store policy." I said. "I am not in charge of the corporate rules." This, of course, is never good enough for them. I have PERSONALLY chosen to forbid them from buying the display! It is my prerogative and joy to tell customers they can't have something so I can get yelled at!

My paycheck. I read that the average retail manager makes $45 an hour. What store is this?!? How do I get in on this amount of money? I worked it out and I think I now make less than I did babysitting in high school (when you account for inflation and annoyance cost).

The Phrase Of Doom. There are a lot of terrible phrases throughout history. Phrases that strike cold terror into the black heart of man. Phrases like, "Hi, I'm Chuckie. Wanna plaaaayyyyy?" But the worst, the all-time worst, is the phrase: "The customer wants to see a manager." This phrase never ends well. It's never a customer coming to compliment me on all the excellent work my team has been doing. It is always customers coming to complain about why I, personally, have decided to discontinue their favorite brand of perfume.

Lack of common sense from customers. People simply don't put two things together until they are on the other end of fitting rooms. For example, one time in my third store, my associate walked into a thigh-high heap of clothes, with no hangers on the bar. Tanya started to process the mound, when she stopped, perturbed. She knew a lot of these items were hung. For some incredibly bizarre reason, a customer took all the clothes OFF THEIR HANGERS to try them on and brought them, hanger-less, back to the fitting room. Tanya had to scavenge fifty hangers throughout the store to put them back out again. Seriously? Why would you do that?

My retail voice. My voice jumps up 8 octaves when I turn on my retail voice. "Oh hiiiiii.... how can I help yoooooooouuuu?" I sound like a cross between Fran Drescher and a mating mouse. It is at the same time insincere and annoying, a whiny parody of actual helpfulness. I think I adapted this as a self-defense mechanism. I am being rude to customers without being outright rude in such a way that they can report me. The minute the customer treats me with respect the voice drops down to a respectable level. If they are rude, the voice gets higher and higher until my voice cracks from all my helpfulness. "Absoolloootly, I would LOOOOVE to help you find that shirt in a different color and different size and smaller collar and tighter fit! Myyyy *crack* pleasure!"

People who dump stuff on the returns counter and stare at you without saying anything. I use my retail voice big-time on these people. "Oh hiiiiiiiiiiiiiii.... do you have a retuuuurrrrnnnnnn today?" Then I will stare at them with a fake smile until they reluctantly nod or grunt assertion. You don't get to get out of talking to me, bucky. If I have to return your stuff you are going to treat me like a person.

The security levels in a retail store. Our store is ridiculous about employee security. We need passwords for EVERYTHING, in case someone is going to break into the register and scan clearance under my name. Not to mention all the passwords must be 10 digits including letters, numbers, special symbols, capitals, no caps, ampersands, a mix of Times New Roman and Helvetica, and an onomatopoeia.[16] This is not the Pentagon. We sell underwear. Chill.

Where my money goes. So I calculated that probably 50% of my salary goes back into my store. Everything I buy is from my store - clothing, housewares, shoes, Easter decorations, etc. Where else would this happen? I can't

---

[16] I chose oink.

imagine employees of McDonald's eat thousands of dollars worth of burgers every month. Well, maybe some of them. They can be pretty chubs.

Overpriced stuff. I now know that everything in every store is vastly overpriced. Retailers mark up their items up to _350 percent_ above the wholesale price. This is very depressing to me. The only perk is a.) I know how much things are really worth, and b.) I am in charge of marking stuff when it goes clearance. Therefore, when I am scanning stuff, I make two piles. "One for customers, one for me! One for customers, one for me!" Not to mention I get an employee discount and a credit card discount. It's gotten to the point where if it is 5 bucks or more, I stick up my nose at it. "6.99? Out of my price range! That's for them rich folks!" I may actually be beating the system. Or at least only paying 50% above the real price instead of 350%. A small win?

Ugly products I am supposed to sell that no one will ever, ever buy. We can tell when buyers are smoking up before making their purchases. Some of the ugliest stuff imaginable enters our doors, certainly not stuff we would ever pick, and then *we're* the ones who have to sell it. We have a game called "Clearance Callout" on truck days. When something arrives on a truck that is particularly hideous, we take bets on when it will go clearance. Leopard lampshades? One month. Sequined booty shorts? A month and a half. Neon pink dress shirts? Surprisingly, over three months. We've had stuff come in on the truck *already marked* clearance. A preemptive suck strike. I have had such ugly items in my store that, true story, I purchased a horrific orange maxi dress and returned it to another store, just to get it out of my sight and into someone else's inventory. I hate receiving items on the truck that I know are going to linger in my store for months, like an unwanted house guest who eats all your food and doesn't match any of your shoes.

Keep in mind that this is the *condensed* list. I started working on this list during my bartending days and kept it going all throughout my retail era. There'll always be annoying people and annoying products. And for some reason I don't have a Things That **Don't** Annoy Me list. It would be too short for publication, I suspect.

Chapter 9

Test Products to Avoid, aka, Don't Use the Mascara

"What you see is that the most outstanding feature of life's history is a constant domination by bacteria."

- Stephen Jay Gould

Listen up, young shoppers. I'm about to impart upon you some very valuable advice. Are you ready? Are you listening? This is very important. All right? Here it is. Big stuff.

Never, I Mean **NEVER**, Use The Beauty Testers.

Did you get that? Was that big enough font? Want me to repeat it?

Never never never never never never never never never never never never never

never never never never never never never
never never never never never never never
never never never never never never never
never never never use the beauty testers.

There is *no* exception to this rule. Beauty
testers are the most disgusting, germ-ridden,
microbe-covered, disease-carrying, spittle-
spattered, and all-around abhorrent things on
our sales floor. This is where bacteria go for a
big sexy orgy.

Elizabeth Brooks conducted a well-
publicized study of makeup testers. Some of the
facts she discovered were, to use the technical
term, grossbuckets. She found that many testers
contain E. Coli, which is a scientific name, to my
understanding, for poop germs. Brooks revealed
that the percentage of tainted tester makeup on
an average day was 43%, and on the busiest day
of the week (Saturday), contamination was
100%. That means *every single item* they tested
was contaminated somehow. Another study
took swabs of over 3,000 beauty items (mascara,
eyeliner, powder, etc) and found 35 types of
bacteria, the majority being of Staphylococcus
aureus, a common cause of skin infections and
respiratory problems. Karen Burke, MD, a

dermatologist in private practice in New York City, says, "You can pick up herpes from a tube of lipstick if a previous user had a cold sore, and conjunctivitis [pinkeye] can be transferred via eye pencils or mascara." Hurrah! Bring out the Q-tips! Let's try on some makeup!

I see all this every day. Teenage girls are the worst about this. They try on every single freaking lipstick we sell, wipe them off their faces, drop the tissues on the ground, and try the same lipsticks on again. They smear blush and bronzer on each other, write swear words on the fixture in eye pencil, lick the lipgloss tips, and put on twelve different colors of eyeshadow, giggling all the while. They will spend upwards of half a day experimenting with makeup, contaminating my entire beauty floor with their young and perky germs, and then waltz out the door looking like younger versions of Tammy Faye Bakker and not a purchase in their pockets. (Except maybe some stolen eyeshadows. Teenage girls are the biggest little kleptomaniacs in the country.[17])

_____

[17] Teenage girls are also notorious for getting makeovers at major department stores before dances and proms and then not buying a single thing. One

Brooks was kind to associates, placing the majority of the blame on customers. Brooks says the testers, "become increasingly contaminated from dirty hands, sneezing, and coughing" over the day from our dirty, dirty customers. "At all the stores we visited, we routinely observed employees disinfecting cosmetic counters and the surface of makeup testers," she says, giving us associates credit for keeping testers clean.

She clearly did not go to my store. I am really, really, really bad about disinfecting makeup testers. Here is my reasoning. (I will put it in haiku form, to make this a cultured and sophisticated book that can be taught in local classrooms.)

As soon as I clean,

Customers will mess it up

Therefore, why do it?

I probably have my team disinfect the beauty testers about once a year. And I am talking about the easy stuff, like sharpening the

---

department store I saw fixed this problem by only making over half a person's face, in theory to show the difference between each side, but really to thwart the teenage mooch problem. Genius!

eye pencils. Spraying alcohol on the lipsticks? You wish. Then there are the items you honestly cannot disinfect. You can't clean the mascara or liquid eyeliner, because the germs are inside the tube. Customers put mascara on their nasty, germ-carrying eyelashes and then put the wand back in the tube. The tube now has a brand new branch of germs added to the bacteria orgy that is already going on. Now they have new, fresh bacteria to reproduce with! Heat up the tiny germ hot tub and bring out the tiny germ waterbeds!

Not only do testers get contaminated, Corporate does not give me a budget to make new testers. Whenever we mark a beauty product out-of-stock to use as a tester, it comes out of our bottom line. One time, one of my new little beauty associates took it upon herself to replace all sixty of our test lipsticks. At $15 each it ended up being a $900 mistake. On slow days we barely break a grand in sales. In one lipstick-stained swoop she annihilated our day's earnings. The District Manager was unamused.

So I scavenge my testers. If you return a lipstick that is mainly unused, you can trust me when I tell you it will be on the sales floor as a tester item the next day. I will swipe disinfectant on the top, check to see no insane person stuck a needle in the center (I read a horror book where that happened, and now can't get it out of my mind. Sorry, now it's in your mind), and pop it onto our full-color "Sunset Rose Lipstick Sparkle and Shine" display. I do the same for eyeshadow, powder, foundation, concealer, blush and bronzer. I do not, however, do that with the mascara or eyeliner, for the reasons stated above. I'm not a total jerk. And I like to avoid pinkeye-based lawsuits.

So very frequently testers are reused returns. And not to gross you out further, but sometimes those purchased items that you think are brand new may be previous returns. Many's been a time when we re-plastic wrapped a new-looking perfume or blush and sneaked it back into the sales floor. Sorry. Sort of.

Some Tips To Avoid The Grossness Of Beauty Testers If You Absolutely Must Use Them Against My Elaborate and Passionate Advice As Well As My Scientific Facts and Poetic Haiku:

- Avoid testing on lips and eyes, which are the most vulnerable to infection; use the back of your hand.

• If you must use beauty testers, avoid the mascara and liquid eyeliner at all costs. Anything where the dispenser is put back in the tube is contributing to the germ party already in progress. Stay away from the germ party. The party favors are herpes and pinkeye.

• Ask the associate for rubbing alcohol or disinfectant to clean the makeup before you try it. Just because we don't *use* the disinfectant doesn't mean we don't *have* it.

• Wash your hands with soap and water or use a hand sanitizer before and after visiting a makeup counter. Coincidentally - we sell hand sanitizer.

• Test only products that come from a shaker or a squeeze or pump dispenser, or those that are single use. Even with this, however, wipe off the dispenser before you use it. People like to touch and handle the dispensers liberally. They're like tactile children at a petting zoo.

• Have an in-store makeup artist apply testers for you.[18] "They are trained by the

---

[18] But not me. Don't bug me.

cosmetic companies to use sanitary measures, including disinfecting their hands, sharpening pencils, and spraying makeup brushes with antibacterial spray between customers," says Cheryl Krebs, a makeup artist at Bloomingdale's in New York City. Clearly Cheryl Krebs is discussing Bloomingdale's and not a standard department store. You ain't getting "sanitary measures training" in my store.

• The best idea: Don't use testers at all, and buy your makeup from a store where you can return it. Inquire about the return policy first.

Unless it's my store. Because I probably rewrapped a return and put it back on the floor.

Chapter 10

Horrors of the Holidays (Back to School = Evil Kids and Christmas = Evil Everyone)

"Fascinatingly confident, rude people are great."

-Steven Moffat

Up to 80% of retail profit comes from the holidays, usually the months of September through mid-January. The two biggest moneymaking times of year are September's Back-to-School (BTS) and of course, December's Christmas/Hanukah/Kwanzaa (XMAS).

I cannot overemphasize how much effort goes into the holiday season. And I cannot overemphasize how miserable the holiday season is for retail associates.

It starts gradually - a fitting room a little busier than usual, a few extra pairs of packaged underwear on the ground. Then it gains momentum, and before you know it you have groups of mothers and kids descending on your

Shoes department, leaving in their wake scattered shoelaces and dirty socks. For Christmas you hear a Christmas carol or two, a few ornaments appear on your truck, and before you know it your store is ripped apart by Christmas gift shoppers, leaving it looking worse than a daisy garden run over by a tank.

I can start a lively conversation with my coworkers discussing which is worse– BTS or XMAS. Both have their downsides and their downsides. I generally prefer BTS. Not only is the destruction isolated to the Kids and Home sections, these are both sections I'm not responsible for. It's ideal. XMAS, on the other hand, attacks the entire store. No section is safe. When people go into frenzied gift–buying mode, everything looks like a gift, including flatware, steam cleaners, sonic toothbrushes, and pantyhose.

Back-to-school's biggest problem, though you would expect it to be, is *not* the children. Although any fixture with merchandise that is kid height stands to be knocked over, unfolded, tossed on the ground, colored and/or drooled on, it is not the kid that I blame. It is the parent, or oftentimes the grandparent, who thinks the destruction of the folded shorts table is just the cutest thing ever.

Some parents are great parents. My best parent story was just last year during the dreaded BTS season. Mom and her two girls were stocking up on clothes the day before most local elementary schools started. I was wandering the store during my closing manager shift when I came to a startled stop and made a small squeak in my throat. Ahead of me was a destructive trail through the middle of the Girls department. You could see the path the woman's kids took, because they were obviously pushing each other into racks and knocking off huge chunks of dresses, t-shirts, leggings, and shorts. It looked like a drunken hippo had lurched its way through a bayou of clothes. I tried to breathe slowly, but it was almost ten at night and my closing associates were going to have to blitz this mess big-time to even have a chance of leaving earlier than midnight.

Ahead of me the girls were screeching and giggling and playing hide-and-go-seek in the piles. They were acting like they had been fed Pixie Stix dipped in Red Bull. I glared at them like Grumpy Cat when the mother came out of the fitting room, pushing the cart in front of her. She looked from me to her kids when her eyes finally landed on the clothes trail, where her eyes widened and she sucked in her breath.

"Janie! Jessie! GET OVER HERE!"

My interest perked. Was she going to grab the kids and make a run for it? That was what all my customers did. But no!

"Did you make this mess?" she demanded to know.

The kids squirmed and looked guiltily away from her. She grabbed the closest one to her. "Did you make this mess?"

Janie, or Jessie, nodded unwillingly. That was enough for the mom.

"I will NOT have children without manners! You will clean this up!"

This was as good as apple pie to me. The kids unhappily started hanging up clothes. But there was more!

"First of all, you will apologize to the lady!" she roared at the Js.

Apple pie and whip cream!

The kids made eye contact with my knees. "Sorry." They mumbled.

The woman went on. "We are terribly sorry, and we realize how inconvenient this is. Can you please explain to my kids why this was such a terrible thing to do?" She pushed the children towards me to listen.

Apple pie, whip cream, with a side of cheesecake.

"Yes *ma'am!*" I said, beaming. "Look, kids, we have to clean up after you. That leads to a lot of trouble on our part. The time we spend cleaning up after you we could use for all sorts of things. We could be putting out new merchandise or re-tagging items. The money the company would save from not picking up after customers can be used to make the prices cheaper for your mom when she is shopping for the two of you. It also makes merchandise dirty for other customers to put on the floor, and it makes a lot more work for us. It's basic manners to always pick up after yourself and not make other people do it for you." The kids looked abashed.

"You have a good mom teaching you good store behavior!" I added.

The mom thanked me. "You aren't done yet, girls," she ordered. "We aren't leaving until this is all picked up." The kids, with a reluctant air, began to pick clothes up off the floor. I shook the mom's hand, nodded to the girls, and left with a spring in my step. We got out on time that night, thanks to the mom with manners.

Sadly though, moms with manners are becoming more and more rare. I see more entitlement in the last couple of years than I did at the beginning of my retail career. Excuse me while I hop on my retail pulpit to self-righteously preach, but every time I see the kids fitting room strewn with clothes I think of what the parents are teaching their kids. My mom would never let me leave a fitting room without hanging up my clothes. The Millennials are already considered self-entitled brats. What are *they* going to teach their kids? Besides trashing fitting rooms, I am shocked when people don't offer to pay for things their kids break (or things *they* break). Or worse, they break something, don't clean up after themselves, and then don't pay for it. Or even worse, people break something, don't clean up after themselves, don't pay for it, and they *don't tell anyone*, so the way we find out that the customer broke a bodywash in the middle of the Beauty section is when an 80-year old woman slips on the slick tile floor, falls and dislocates both her knees in a puddle of plumeria.

However, generations have a tendency to do the opposite of the generation before them. So maybe it will come full-circle and the Millennials' kids will be thoughtful, considerate adults who clean out their fitting rooms. And maybe lions will become vegetarians.

Okay, off the pulpit. It was getting preachy up there.

So besides fitting room messes during BTS, we get the over-attached parents shopping with the new college freshmen. These parents are very concerned their sons and daughters get the best quality dorm room gear, in an attempt to take care of their dear darling offspring when they are far from home. I hate to tell them that the expensive down comforter they just purchased will have more vomit on it by the second half of rush week than the fur of a bulimic Tasmanian devil.

The best part of BTS is that everything goes clearance a few days after the kids actually go back to school. So if you hold out long enough you get some killer deals on kid's clothes, bedding, and school supplies. All my associates hold out for this. I've had associates quit the day after they do a clearance spending spree. As long as they make it through the holidays I don't care. It is very hard to hold on to associates after they experience their first holiday season.

The reason for that is we hire a majority of people to do one job. And this is the absolute worst job in the store. Worse than a deep-sea diver in a sewage plant, worse than a lifeguard at that *Jaws* beach, worse than being Lindsey Lohan's PR director, worse than Phil Spector's stylist. The one job in the store that you could never pay me enough to do ever, but especially during the holidays, is ....

Cashier.

The poor cashiers have the worst job of all jobs, bar none. You think I'm kidding? Because clearly this is such a brilliantly funny humor book? I'm exceedingly serious on this front. Cashiers are expected to be:

-Greeters (*'Hello! Hi there! How are you! Welcome! Glad you're here!' Repeat*)

-Store Maps (*'Where are the Shoes? Where is Customer Service? Where is that one pink top I saw three months ago in another store?'*)

-Politicians (*'Yes, I see you think you are next in line, but this gentleman believes he is. Let's start a dialogue'*)

-Angels (*Completely joyful and friendly at all times with all people, exuding a halo of pure calm and serenity*)

-Punching Bags (*Expected to endure all abuse for things completely beyond their control, such as the dress the customer wants is not in stock in her size*)

-Psychologists (*'So...you think you should be able to get everything you want without question? Let's talk about your mother and how she instilled this Napoleonic complex in you'*)

-Speed Scanners (*Should average thousands of items an hour, no matter how big the item is, where the item's tags are, or even if the tags exist. Customers have things to do!*)

-Project Managers (*Made to fold, hang, and do any stupid repetitive job while popping their heads up to look at the register every five seconds, like they are auditioning for Meerkat Manor, to see if a customer has ambled up whenever they are distracted for a millisecond*)

-Loss Prevention Specialists ('*Let me make sure all hard tags are off, soft tags deactivated, perfume boxes opened, right shoe matches left shoe matches shoebox, oh, alarm went off? Let me check everything again.*')

All of this smiling, greeting, exuding calm, avoiding conflict - while getting paid eight dollars an hour.

To add insult to injury, no matter how many times I stock their registers, they are somehow always left with broken crayons and a red pen that doesn't work. "Here you go, sir. Fill out your check with your choice of crayon. Burnt Sienna or Mauve-elous?"

All you cute little applicants who like people, you must avoid being the cashier. I watch new cashiers, sweet, happy, innocent cashiers who begin one day as a ringer and end up later a broken, bitter, nasty employee. This process can happen in less than a week.

This horrible job is ten times worse during the holidays. During the slow season cashiers can go for hours without dealing with a customer. They absent-mindedly dust fixtures and wait patiently for the one customer in the store on a Tuesday afternoon to come to their register to buy two small candy bars. During the holidays you don't stop ringing for a minute. God help you if you need to take a break. You had better be at the end of your line or you will get body-slammed back into your register by an impatient soccer mom.

Cashiers get the brunt of the holiday joy. They get scolded by religious groups for saying Happy Holidays, even though it is a corporate mandate and not their choice. They cut their fingers on broken Seahawks ornaments. They constantly try to drown out the overhead Christmas music loop and gag on the Cinnamon Apple Pine Wonderland candle scents. Counterintuitively, the only real upside of the holidays in retail is: you get more hours to deal with all the holiday crud. Ironic.

We all have to work 6 to 7 days a week, no exceptions. It's a law of retail. So we spend 60 to 70 hours a week in December throwing merchandise off trucks into the arms of demanding gift buyers, only to spend 60 to 70 hours a week in January taking back that same merchandise as returns. Paychecks boom for a few brief weeks and then drop off the cliff on January 16th.

We start preparing for the holiday season in June. Holiday music starts playing in October. Customers start complaining about the holiday setup in November. It happens every year. As the music starts playing and associates hang the Christmas ornaments, customers chime in an annoying chorus, "Oh no, it's way too early for Christmas! You shouldn't start advertising Christmas yet!" Listen, you people, 1.) I have no control over a billion-dollar profit, country-wide retail chain's decisions, and 2.) Why are you always so surprised when Christmas comes around? It happens every year.[19] Accept it. Embrace it.

---

[19] Unless the Grinch steals it. I'd be poor Macy-Lou Who.

Of course the pinnacle, the zenith, that cherry on top of the sales sundae is .... Black Friday. Black Friday is the hands-down biggest sales day of the year. It's called Black Friday because it's traditionally the day of the year that retailers get back in the black.[20] So in one day we can do more sales than the previous ten months. It's no wonder retailers push the start time back further and further each year to get more mileage from this day.

Most associates despise Black Friday, but I adore it. Truly, I adore everything about it. It's complete and utter chaos from the moment midnight hits the end of Thursday night until twelve AM Saturday morning, and you can't be bored for a minute.

You start your day at 3am. After driving to the store, you exit your car groggily holding your coffee. As you walk to the store, you see a huge crowd of people in the pitch darkness, many in sleeping bags. The droves are waiting impatiently for the doors to open, passing

---

[20] Fun fact #1 – The biggest sales day of the year is Black Friday. Fun Fact #2 - The 2nd biggest day is the Saturday before Christmas. In case you ever play the retail version of Trivial Pursuit.

around ads and discussing their all-day Black Friday sales tactics. Holding your coffee aloft, you push through them to the doors as they spot you and surge like wildebeests, shouting and pointing at the ad, "Where is the 42-inch TV?!? WHERE?!?"

If you make it through the mob, you are greeted by seventy-five members of your staff. The majority of your staff is scheduled for those first ten hours because those are the crucial sales hours. The remaining fifteen people on your crew are stuck on cleanup duty. All of your associates *will* be working Black Friday. There is no excuse to calling out on Black Friday. You had better be dead if you call out on Black Friday or you will be when you walk in on Saturday.

You walk past the majority of your merchandise on your way to the back. Almost all your merch is on the floor, with the remainder piled on carts in the stock room for replenishment. We prepare for Black Friday months ahead of time, making special piles of items featured in the ad, and filling U-boats (see Chapter 12: Tools of The Trade) with toys, toys, and more toys. Our store is not known for our toy selection, but when Black Friday Fever hits it doesn't matter what the item is, it matters that it's on sale.

You set your team to go out before the doors open, answering questions and selling your in-store credit card while you have a captive audience. This is the best way to start your day. You will find a nice-looking family group and say with great, cheery enthusiasm, "Good morning! How are you all doing today?" In which the nice-looking mother will reply, "We were doing fine until these five b*tches cut in front of us." Yay! Black Friday joy! This will lead to a huge brawl where your boss will then come out and threaten to send everyone home. "Do you want to go home? Do you? You behave or no shopping for you!" With sulky faces they will agree to behave.

After that cheerful exchange, you get back inside and do your final walk-through, the throng pounding on the windows outside, waiting for 4am to hit. You run over your list in your mind, making sure you've checked off all your prep items. Your team is ready at the get-go, your store is perfectly neat, clean, and stocked. The clock turns from 3:59 to 4:00. You nod to your cashiers to open the doors.

YeeeeeeeeeeeeOOOOOOWWWWWW the crowd stampedes in like a herd of frantic cats, yowling and scattering throughout the store, desperately scratching and pushing each other out of the way in an attempt to find the best items from the ad. The store turns from a peaceful lounge to a crazed, manic retail rave.

Most people were shocked to hear about the Walmart security guard who was trampled to death during a Black Friday's opening. I was not. I'm honestly shocked it doesn't happen more often. With the insanity I see every year, I can't believe our store has escaped any major bodily injuries to our customers or to associates.

Customers shriek at associates who are frantically trying to both stay out of the way and help everyone who needs help. The professional

Black Friday shoppers (I'll call them the Black Ops Friday Team), have already mapped out all their operations for the entire day, complete with blueprints of all the major stores, headsets, and walkie-talkies to communicate with their escape vehicle. The Black Ops Friday people are my favorite. You can overhear them barking to each other, "This is Black Hawk Five. I've got Dora's Talking Treehouse! Do you have the animated fish tank yet? We'll reconvene at Register 4 at 1200 hours exactly. *What do you mean* Red Fox is down in luggage? We've got to get to Pier One before Power Hours end!" These operatives will be in and out of your store in less than twenty minutes. They have already plotted the exact three products they're going to hit, and they will dash, grab, buy, and be out your door and onto the next store before the first ambler makes it to the store map.

The Black Ops Friday team has been discussing Black Friday all Thanksgiving day. One professional Black Ops Friday member told me she shops for 16 hours on Black Friday and hits over 20 stores - Macy's, JC Penney, Nordstrom, Costco, the Apple Store, Chico's, and Kohl's were just the beginning of her list. Her husband waits outside in the car with his laptop, car charger, eight DVDs, and a cooler of sandwiches and granola bars so they don't waste any precious time getting food. I didn't ask if there was a restroom in the car.

Even the non-professional shoppers don't mess around on Black Friday. They urgently power-dash through the aisles, pushing each other aside even if they aren't one hundred percent sure what they're looking for. (Secret sales tip: if you want to sell something lame, grab a couple of associates and huddle around an item talking and gesturing excitedly. Customers will shove through you, grab whatever it is and buy it on the spot, even if it sucks. **Excellent** way to get rid of your leftover Duck Dynasty camouflage bath towels.)

So this frantic shopping continues throughout the day, the crowd eating up the merchandise like a flock of ravenous locusts. My pretty Justin Bieber fragrance fixture is annihilated and my carefully stacked tower of telescopes is destroyed, half-opened telescopes thrown across the store, like a typhoon just went through Copernicus's Observatory. Whatever the must-have item of the year is is sold out by 4:15 AM, leaving you to fend off hundreds of angry customers who came in specifically for that item. The best technique is to try to sell them on something similar. This was really tough the year of the ZhuZhu pets. I would tell customers, "Well, no, we don't have the speed-racing stuffed hamsters that you can dress in little costumes, but we do have ....Matchbox cars! We'll put a Barbie cowgirl hat on the pink one!"

My favorite Black Friday fad item was the Snuggie. Do you remember the year of the Snuggie? Snuggies were the must-have item, more popular than Furbies and Sea Monkeys combined. We had blue Snuggies, pink Snuggies, white Snuggies, camo Snuggies, Elmo Snuggies, school colors Snuggies–a veritable ocean of Snuggies. If we put all the Snuggies together spread out across the country, we could've covered California to New York in tacky cheap material.

It was Snuggie-topia (SnugFest?). We had huge tables devoted to Snuggies. When we ran out of a certain color customers placed voodoo hexes on us. The power of a fad is overwhelming, and retailers coast on those fads until the trend wave crashes and we little salespeople are left dashed and waterlogged on the shore, spare slap bracelets scattered about us on the sand like seaweed.

Now every register in the store is ringing nonstop. Each register has a cashier and a bagger, designed to maximize efficiency and minimize customer wait time. Managers prowl up and down the aisles, giving directions to customers, helping fix associate screw-ups, and keeping breaks on track. All stores have a complicated breaking system, because if you think you are shutting down one of the registers for an associate to take a break, then you unwisely do not fear death by customers. Several associates will be assigned solely as breakers who make complex loops throughout the store to ensure our cashiers, jewelry associates, and customer service associates all get their 15- and 30-minute breaks.

When it is finally your break time, you make your way to the back. You have packed your emergency snack and water bottle to prepare for your all-day adventure, because as an associate, once you get into the store, you are stuck. Your 15-minute break has to be taken inside the store. Even if you take off your name tag to avoid being mobbed by the crazed consumers, there is no way you can push through the throng, get outside, do what you need to do, and be back in in 15 minutes. Therefore, stores always hire caterers to bring food in for all the associates.

Now, I have more retail wisdom to impart. While you must never volunteer to host the holiday party (more on this later), you should *always* volunteer to be in charge of Black Friday food. This is the best job possible. Local restaurants, in a desperate attempt to win your large order, will bring in stacks of food for you to sample. It's awesome. For a full week I don't have to bring in lunch. Monday the Mexican restaurant brings me taquitos, Tuesday the rib restaurant brings me brisket, Wednesday the sandwich place brings me turkey, ham, and veggie subs. It's like I am a high school athlete being courted by the NCAA, food–wise.

So the Black Friday chaos continues non-stop for hours. Lines wrap around the store, sometimes lapping each other twice. You'll immediately run out of carts and bags, but don't worry - people will use the store wheelchairs, designated for your paraplegic or injured customers, to tote around their Bluetooth stereo systems and Memory Foam mattress pads. Line greeters direct the traffic to the open registers like the dancing policeman, but with less rhythm. The overhead music is muted under the sounds of arguing, squealing, laughing, discussing, and walkie-talkie static. The temperature of the store rises degree by degree until we crank the AC up to counteract the body heat.

At about three in the afternoon the crowds will slowly start to ebb. Gradually, your customers will finish their checkouts and disperse onto the next sale. With a grateful sigh, you stretch your arms and relax for the first time in over ten hours. Then you look around at what the locusts have left. On the plus side, you've sold so much that half of all your shelves are empty. On the negative side, the other half of the shelves is an annihilated mess. The store looks like you told a thousand kindergartners that there were free kittens hidden in the store and set them loose with cat treats.

Here is more retail advice–always volunteer to work the *first* black Friday shift. The chaos is the fun part. The cleaning up is the non-fun part. It is a delight to pass the keys over to the cleanup crew and let them put back together what the customers tore apart. You get to leave behind the worst recovery shift of the year. The only good part in the night shift is that you are not expected to get the store up to a high level of recovery, or even a half-assed level of recovery, because everyone saw what you were left with. And you don't have to put away half of the merchandise because it walked out your doors that morning.

After the locusts leave, you will give a report to your DM comparing this year's sales to last year's sales. Black Friday sales have not been quite as successful as they used to be due to online shopping. Most retailers give the same deals online as they do in store while providing free shipping, and then they are surprised when sales traffic drops in stores. It's like the newspapers. I imagine the major newspaper editors' conversation. "We will give customers all the news online and provide them with exclusive, unlimited free content. And then...the customers will buy the paper copy! Yes! It's a foolproof plan!"

After the store is destroyed and the sales report is in, then, and only then, are you permitted to stumble home. You walk into the parking lot, squinting in the sun, and try to remember where you parked 14 hours ago. Finally locating your car, you lurch inside, turn the key, and drive home, windows open and music blasting to keep you from passing out at the wheel. If you make into the house, you'll fall asleep into the deepest, sweetest, after-sale sleep you have ever had. If you don't make into the house, you will awaken on your front walkway, snuggling your outdoor light post, as interested dogs investigate the scent of thousands of people and products that cover your jeans.

Another successful Black Friday.

After Black Friday ends, so begins the 33 Days of Christmas. Although technically it's already been the past Four Months of Christmas. Every day brings more and more sales, until the Saturday before Christmas when it reaches fever pitch. Christmas is a frenzied freak fest of consumption. "But Macy," you say, "You big complainer, holidays pay the bills!" And you are right.[21] Busy times keep us all employed. And I'm grateful to the many generous people who buy gifts for their friends, family, coworkers, and service providers.

At least until all the returns come back to my store.

---

[21] You know-it-all.

Chapter 11

The Fun Calendar and Captain Fun

"When the whole world is crazy, it doesn't pay to be sane."

-Terry Goodkind

Corporate is always coming up with new, cutesy programs in an attempt to distract Associates from the suckiness of their jobs. The biggest program is the "Fun Calendar." Corporate will design a calendar of adorably nauseating events that are meant to motivate associates and involve them in company loyalty. Because nothing makes you more loyal to your company than wearing wacky socks while customers yell at you.

The common consensus among Associates is that Corporate should take the money that is spent on calendar design and put it towards our paychecks, but Corporate knows better. People aren't motivated by *money*. People are motivated by *fun!*

I got to experience the fun firsthand when I was ~~chosen as tribute~~ given the opportunity to be in charge of the Fun Calendar. I was "Captain Fun." Not only was I assigned to fine-tune the Corporate calendar, I was told to make colorful posters, fancy flyers, and notices for huddles so that everyone would know to partake in the Fun.

The glory of this job is that it is a lot of extra, unpaid work, and, as an added bonus, everybody hates you. It's the same situation as being in charge of the holiday party.[22] One year I volunteered to host the holiday party.[23] With great ambition and enthusiasm, I decided to go all out. I chose a nice local bowling alley and I made the party Hollywood-themed. Overspending my budget and chipping in some of my own money, I threw the biggest bonanza in my store's history! The walls were festooned with celebrity photos. From the ceiling dangled gold stars, and the floor was covered with a red carpet. The tables were covered in candy and

---

[22] Never volunteer to run the holiday party.

[23] See footnote above.

popcorn buckets. The associates were given top hats or boas as they entered, and were directed to a photo booth where they could take photos of themselves in front of the Hollywood sign. In the left corner of the alley were free chair massages, on the right, buckets of tokens they could use to play unlimited arcade games. Themed music from famous films played overhead. Kids and spouses were invited and everyone was given pizza, soda, and slices of a huge cake that said, "Thanks For All Your Hard Work, Team!" All of this was free of charge and lasted over five hours, in which people ate, drank, and bowled to their hearts' content. So of course you can imagine what happened.

People complained because the prize machine for the tokens was broken.

Seriously, never host the holiday party.

But getting back to the Fun Calendar. Corporate had a real tendency to overbook the days in the fun calendar. This is a mistake because Associates get confused on which day is what, leading to a Monday morning with one associate wearing school colors, one in jeggings, and several in Pimps & Hos costumes.[24]

It is amazing how involved some people got with the dress-up days. Most associates dial in their four-hour shift and hurry home, but there are always a few truly passionate employees who have no life other than the store. These are the people that truly care about the quality of their Tim Gunn costumes.

Halloween is the biggest fun costume day, of course. The casual costumers wear cat ears and witch hats, while the hard-core few dress in their handmade, home-sewn Pikachu costumes. The women like to push the envelope at Halloween as well. The dress code at my store for the majority of the time is pretty strict. We don't allow skorts for some reason, even though you can't tell the difference between a skirt and a skort. There is an extensive byline that warns against wearing clothes that are too short, too low-cut, or too suggestive.[25] Apparently this all

---

[24] This was actually never an option. Woulda been sweet if it was, though.

[25] They address this to both men and women. In case Wally from the Shoe Department wears his weekend short-shorts, which he has been known to do.

goes to hell on Halloween. Female associates wear the sluttiest costumes I have even seen, and they wear them on the sales floor. Fishnets and garters abound. We can't complain though. Our sales always go up when the associate dressed as a slutty librarian works the Men's Basics department.

As Captain Fun, I get scolded if my costume is not fun and festive enough. The trouble is that I'm a manager too. Imagine how well it goes over when I receive a territory manager visit wearing my feetie pajamas. In case your company does not have a Fun Calendar,[26] let me show you a sample:

---

[26] Lucky.

FUN CALENDAR

SUN	MON	TUE	WED	THUR	FRI	SAT
1 School Spirit Sunday	2 Wear Your Shirt Inside Out!	3 Pajama Jammie Jam	4 Wacky Sox Wed	5 Rhapsody of Red	6 Gala of Green	7 Parade of Puce
8 Silly Hat Sunday	9 Dress Like Your Favorite Animated Rodent Day	10 Scare A Friend Day BOO!	11 Pretend You Are In Paris	12 Pretend You Are Anywhere but Here	13 Dress like Twins and Triplets	14 Bring Your Kid to Work Day
15 50's Day! 50's	16 60's Day! 60's	17 70's Day! 70's	18 80's Day! 80's	19 90's Day! 90's	20 00's Day! 00's	21 Future Day! Future
22 Princes and Princesses	23 Represent Your Area Code Monday (206)	24 Christmas In July	25 Dress Like Your Favorite Thundercat	26 Tribble and Squeegee Gear	27 Hobbit Feet Friday	28 Be Your Favorite Reality Show Star

Ooo, child, you wish you worked at my store now, don't you?

The best Fun Calendar day is Bring Your Kid to Work Day, because we actually make the kids work. No joke. It is awesome, free labor. They are all too young to realize how soul-crushingly boring it all is and treat it like a fun adventure. One year we had them sort all 5,000 of the mixed-up sales signs in the stock room (none of *us* sure wanted to do it), and one year we had them bagging merchandise at the registers for the cashiers. Child labor laws go amiss on Bring Your Kid to Work Day.

The worst Fun Calendar Day is School Spirit Day. Whatever school you root for is going to be the sworn enemy of someone else's school. This goes for your elementary schools as well. The East Mercer Apples hate the Lakeside Learnin' Leapfrogs. So you go through the day in your school shirt and fend off countless jokes/thinly veiled threats. I get enough animosity from customers every day. I don't need school rivalry to help it along.

The most ironic Fun Calendar day is Christmas in July Day. It's already Christmas in July. It's been Christmas since June. Seeing everyone dressed in reindeer antlers and Santa hats is only a cruel premonition of the evil that awaits us. It's like a mini-shower of raindrops before the monsoon hits. We know it's coming to destroy our lives. Why taunt us?

To wrap up this Chapter O' Fun, I leave you with more advice. You should volunteer to run fun calendars like you should volunteer to run the holiday party.[27] These are jobs that win you no respect, no extra money, and no dignity. Don't let your boss sweet-talk you into these jobs. The reason he is sweet-talking you is because *he* doesn't want to do it. This shows he's smart enough to be the boss.

But if one day you truly want to put on your Lion-O costume during Thundercat Day, feel free to go for it. Sometimes, as long as you aren't in charge, now and then a Fun Calendar day can actually be fun.[28]

---

[27] Never volunteer to run the holiday party.

[28] Don't tell Corporate, or I will volunteer you to be Captain Fun next year.

Chapter 12

Tools of the Trade

"A poor workman blames his tools."

-Proverb

Quick– define these sentences. "I need you to grab an RF and rolling rack to prep for the new marks. Make sure the new juniors merch is hard tagged and the backstock is spiderwrapped."

Did you understand that? Congrats, you work retail.[29] If that sentence sounded like ancient Valyrian, I have provided a translation of all the tools of the retail trade.

---

[29] Why?

U-Boats

U-Boats are big carts shaped like, you guessed it, an F. Just kidding. They are shaped like a U and are used to transport merchandise that can't be hung. U-Boats move housewares, shoeboxes, and folded clothes all throughout the store, and they are also excellent late-night go-carts when the stores close and the Retail Racing Derby begins down the Intimates aisle.[30]

Z-Rails/Rolling Racks

Rolling racks are commonly used in retail to move merchandise, aka merch, around. They

---

[30] Personal high score - 7 seconds from Home to Juniors!

are metal bars on wheels that can fit about 200 pieces of merchandise. Rolling racks are used to transport merchandise from the trucks to the floor, organize merchandise off of tangled racks, and often used to hide go-backs from the district manager when he visits. Rolling racks are convenient tools for trucks, clearance marks, and fitting rooms. They are also amazingly adept at locating the most painful part of your ankle to attack when you pull them into departments behind you.

Fitting Room Bars

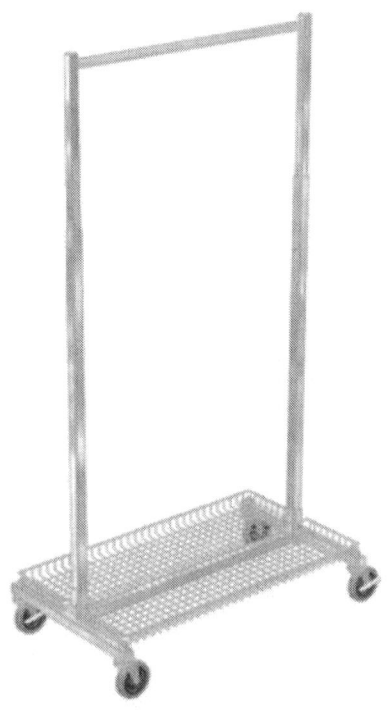

Fitting room bars have been designed and redesigned in an effort to make them more efficient. They are usually mini-versions of the rolling racks that are tucked into fitting rooms. At the end of the day, the fitting room bars are dump racks. "I don't want it! Put it away for me!"

In some smart stores, there are limits to what you are allowed in and out of the fitting rooms. Attendants hand you a plastic number for how many items you have, and you must bring the exact number of items back out again. This is technically for theft, I think, but it helps with fitting room nightmares. Customers have accountability and have to look the attendant in the eye when they bring out their items. It is much more difficult to be a jerk when someone is staring at you while you do it.

Our store, of course, lets you take as much as you want and leave as much as you want (on the floor).

Callboxes

Callboxes abound in most big box retail stores. Press them, and like magic an associate won't appear. Callboxes are supposed to make up for our lack of payroll and staffed employees on the floor, however, since we have no one on the floor to help you in the first place, we definitely don't have anyone available to traipse over to a callbox.

The design flaw our team made is the buttons are *perfect* kid height. They could not have designed anything more appealing to a small bored shopper. On busy days, I feel like I'm on the Scavenger Hunt from Hell, chasing one call box after the other throughout the store. Pressing the button always creates a pleasant bell tone and a lady stating the name of the department that needs help.

Ding! "Misses Please!" *Ding* "Men's Please!" *Ding* "Shoes Please!"

If you don't make it in time, the bell increases to ringing twice, creating a frantic Pavlovian effect on all of us, scrambling across the tiled floor, tongues hanging out and panting in our desperate rush to lurch to and swat the "off" button.

Ding Ding! "Misses Please!" *Ding Ding!* "Men's Please!" *Ding Ding!* "Shoes Please!"

By the time it gets to the dreaded triple ring, you might as well disconnect the boxes and go home for the day. You've been thwarted by 6-year-olds.

<u>Registers</u>

Most retail registers at big companies are becoming more sophisticated. They've gone from Grandma and Grandpop's Old-Tyme Country Store registers:

To ultra-sleek, sophisticated touchscreens:

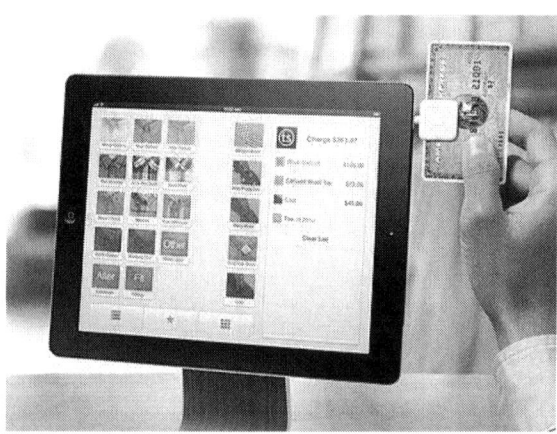

We benefit from some pretty fancy registers, and after years at my company I'm pretty savvy on the old POS system. (Yes, it's called POS. For Point-of-Sale. What were you thinking, you dirty little reader?) I can change a price, scan a credit card, open a charge account, and check complete in 90 seconds or less. It's pretty great, and I have some experience for comparison.[31]

Nevertheless, they have their flaws. The biggest one is that corporate does not trust its little cashier minions to make a lot of decisions. (Which is probably a good idea, in all fairness. See Chapter 3). Thus, the manager on duty is requested to turn a key to authorize countless stupid transactions at all hours of the day. I don't even ask why I am turning the key anymore. The cashier will start, "Macy, this customer needed a price change...." and I will interrupt, "Don't care." and go back to my job. I

---

[31] I used to bartend and we had the worst possible registers. One of my co-workers was fired because we would name the tables to keep track of our parties, and one day at random our prehistoric register system started printing the names on the receipts. The table of "Mean Ol' B*tches" was not amused.

have probably authorized multiple illegal employee price-markdowns. Oh well. Loss Prevention can figure it out.[32]

One of my greatest passive-aggressive joys is when I close down registers. People see me standing behind the register, and therefore assume I'm open. As I'm counting down pennies, I wait patiently for my prey to approach. When they are a foot away, I whip my head up with a big fake smile and say loudly, "She can help you right around the corner!" I then snap my head back down and continue counting. This is one of the only times I'm allowed to blow a customer off, and I absolutely love it.

Hard Tags/Spider Wraps

There are two types of thieves in the retail world: the professional criminals, and the opportunists. The professional criminals are the ones with the toolkit for removing tags, the coupon crime rings, and the getaway car waiting outside. The opportunists are the stupid thirteen-year-olds who see a pair of panties and think it will be easy to stuff it in their purses.

---

[32] Or they can suck it. You'll find out in the next chapter how much I hate Loss Prevention.

Hard tags and spider wraps are no deterrence to the professionals, but will thwart the little opportunists (at least some of the time). The problem with hard tags and spider wraps is they take a big fat chunk of our time to put them on, making floor associates hate them.[33]

Hard Tags look like this:

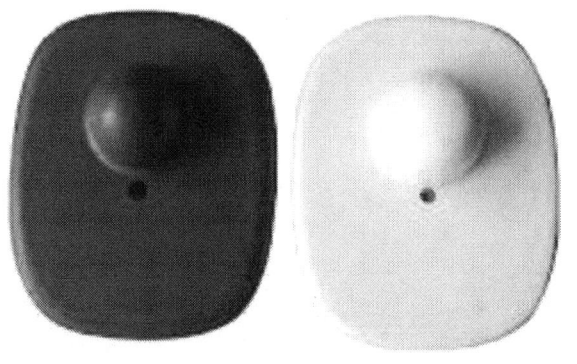

---

[33] Along with hating Loss Prevention. Have I mentioned that I hate Loss Prevention?

Spider Wraps look like this:

Both beep when they go through this:

This would be a foolproof criminal-catching plan except the towers beep

ALL. THE. TIME.

I mean, one out of every two customers will set it off because they have cell phones in their purses. Kids will set it off dragging their toys too close to it. Carts will set it off because of the metal in the wheels. Therefore, our cashiers (who as you know are the gatekeepers of all and are simultaneously doing ten jobs at once) are less than inclined to investigate every beep. So even if your purse is filled with fifty panties and you set off the towers, chances are the harried cashier will wave you off with a distracted glance and return to ringing/hanging clothes/directing traffic/talking on the walkie/managing complaints.

So as you can see, hard tags and spider wraps are useless and annoying and don't work. They are the Kardashians of the security world.

Carts

Carts are an everyday hassle. Constant cart complaints include:

"Where is the cart with the kid's seat??"

"What do you mean all the carts are in use??"

"Why is this cart all wet??"

Carts get as disgusting as fitting rooms. When people take out carts, they transition the mentality that the cart is temporarily theirs, and thus they are free to destroy it. I shudder at the end of the night when I reach in to the bottom of a cart and pull out a sticky soda can, nasty balled-up tissues, and crushed Cheerios by the hundreds.

Carts also like to migrate all over town. They are like pigeons, flocking away from the roost, and you have to call them to fly home at the end of the night. However, we do not have a very sophisticated cart retrieval system. My cart retrieval system is looking outside, seeing it's a sunny day, and announcing over the walkie, "I'm going to do a cart run!" I then take a good twenty minutes to carouse the parking lot searching for "lost carts" and sunning myself. Cart runs are also favorites of the smokers. If an associate announces every couple of hours they are doing a cart run, you can rest assured your carts *are* being retrieved: in between inhalations.

Collections

Collections are assortments of outfits meant to work together. There's a few tops, bottoms, dresses, usually in the same color palette, or with some of the bizarre designers, similar sequin and/or ruffle palette. Department stores are a big mess of collections, usually from some recent celebrity who has decided to begin their own clothing line in an attempt to become relevant. This is also the tactic they take when they start their own perfume lines with fragrances like "Fragrant Mist" which actually smell like "Yak Fur."

My favorite part of the collections is the names. All the names sound like they have been ejected from the Pretentious Phrase Generator (Dave Barry discovered this machine at wineries where they describe wine). Some examples of this are Obscure Garden, Smokey Cityscape, and Mystical Circus. These are real collection names in my store. They'll take an ostentatious adjective and combine it with a useless noun, and voilà! Runway fashion!

Anyone can do the job of the Pretentious Phrase Generator. Here! Even you can try! Get your little pen out and play some mix-n-match!

<u>Ostentatious Adjective</u>................... <u>Useless Noun</u>

Sensual... Shadows
Gossamer.. Jungle
Burnished .... Skyline
Static... Illusion
Satin... Garden
Opal.. Lust
Silken.. History

Theoretical	Theater
Noir	Porpoise
Flowy	Pirouette
Chartreuse	Morgue
Puce	Apocalypse

With just a few pen strokes, you can name your own collection. Opal Illusion! Gossamer Jungle! Sensual Porpoise!

I could rock the collection-naming job.

Now you have an overview of the tools of the retail trade. You know the secret lingo and thus you can work in retail, where you live a glorious, pampered life with piles of benefits, a company car, and all the respect you've ever craved. Would I lie to you?[34]

---

[34] I'm not going to answer that.

Chapter 13

Loss Prevention, or Don't Steal! (But if You Do, You Won't Get Caught)

"Opportunity makes a thief."

-Francis Bacon

Let's do the math here. My store is open 8am until 10pm, and occasionally 11 pm or midnight. We are *never* open for less than that. That means we are continually open for 14 hours a day or more, times 7, equals 98 hours a week.

A Loss Prevention supervisor works 36 hours a week. Therefore, he/she is around approximately 35% of the time or less. And the majority of that time is spent on busywork and paper wrangling. So the store is actually being watched maybe *10% of all open hours.*

What this means is the Weasels have a VERY small chance of getting caught.

The Weasels are the thieves of retail, and the Typical Weasel Maneuvers are many.[35] They switch tags from cheap clothes to expensive clothes. They peel clearance stickers off clearance and stick them on the tags of premium, hundred-dollar dress pants. They stick tags behind mirrors, under the fitting room carts, and in the pockets of jeans. I have seen an LP officer in a fitting room slit open a seat cushion with a razor and pull out a pile of tags from inside the stuffing. The thief had cut the seat cushion open, stuck tags in, and re-sewn the cushion.

Weasels carry toolkits, complete with pliers to tear off hard security tags, scissors to cut out soft monitor tags, and their own ticketing gun to re-ticket clothes. They are exceedingly crafty and tremendously clever. Well, some of them.

My first year of retail, I considered myself on par with a homicide detective. I was confident I would deter any thief, and should I not be able to deter them, I would call the police,

---

[35] Get this - a group of weasels is a sneak. A sneak of weasels. How perfect is that?

point the Weasel out, and say in a confident police chief tone, "Take him away, boys!" I took every pair of jeans or Dyson vacuum that was stolen to be a personal affront.

Seven years later, I could care less if anyone steals anything. It's LP's problem. This has contributed to less-than-cordial relationships with LP now. It doesn't help that within the first few minutes of meeting new LP officers I mention, "By the way, LP is very low on my list of priorities." I have disliked every LP officer I have ever worked with after my first experience. These wannabe cops are whiny little babies who call their boss at the first sign of trouble.

In stores, Loss Prevention is known as Loss Reaction. There is very little preventing. Should a customer steal something, Loss Prevention has to ask him, "Please sir, can you stick around until the cops come?" LP has no gun, weapon, cuffs, or any other equipment for detaining; all they can do is request. This works okay on terrified 12-year-olds, but not so much on seasoned thieves. More than once I've watched LP sprint across the parking lot only to skid to a stop a few feet from the thief, gesturing and pointing to the store, as the thief hops into the getaway car and takes off. "Stick around until the cops come? I'm going to... NOT do that."

The Loss Prevention employees are the only ones who may monitor and/or approach a thief. Employees are told in no uncertain terms never to attempt to stop someone who is trying to steal. It has to do with lawsuits and responsibility. If you try to stop a criminal and get shot, the cost to the company is going to be a whole lot more than the cost of a stolen vacuum cleaner.

In 2011 at a Walmart in Utah, a Weasel stuck a Netbook up under his shirt. A Walmart employee asked him to come to the back where three other employees were waiting. The Weasel brandished a handgun and ran for the door, where the employees tackled him and grabbed the gun away from him, recovering the merchandise while the crowd cheered.

Heroes, right?

Not so much. The employees were fired after management said they violated company policy by disarming an alleged shoplifter who had pulled a gun inside the store.

The stores make it very clear. It's not our job to chase the bad guys. This fact, combined with one of my first Loss Prevention experiences, has led me to my current OK-Fine-Steal-Stuff-But-Please-Throw-The-Tags-Away-So-I-Don't-Have-to-Clean-Them-Up attitude.

My first LP experience was a typical apprehension. While I hate the Weasels and often plot for their demise, I also have a problem: the minute anyone cries, I absolve them from everything. This has been a problem throughout my whole career. If an associate comes in after ten tardies and twenty customer complaints, I am bona-fide ready to throw their booties into the street. Then the minute the associate's face turns up to me with a quivering lip and tear-filled eyes, I cave like a Chilean mineshaft. "NO, we won't fire you! NO, it's okay that you were late! NO, it's okay you swore at that customer's children! Please don't cry!"

With that background, I present to you the story that ended my career in criminal justice.

If the Bras Don't Fit, You Must Acquit

My LP officer had stopped a woman and sat her in the office for shoplifting. She was somewhere in her twenties, a hoochy-mama in too-tight jeans, with worse teeth than an English bar wench. The officer called me in to be a witness.

The woman was in all-out hysterics. Her comments went something like this: "Oh please please please don't call the police, this is the first time I've done anything like this, I have two kids, hey I know the mayor and I'll tell him about this and you'll get in trouble, oh please forgive me, um, actually, I have eight kids, they need a mom, please mister, I will never come into the store again oh I promise, no I SWEAR!"

Max sneered at her. "I don't think so. The police are on their way. Sit tight." He continued to enter in her information into the computer from her driver's license, impartial to her tears.

I sat in the chair, squirming. Wasn't Max being awfully unsympathetic?

This probably really was her first time. She was obviously terrified.

In fact, he was being really pretty mean. Maybe I should say something. Let him know that he's way out of line.

The woman sat slumped forward in the chair. Her head was in her hands and I could hear her muffled whimpers through her fingers.

Max picked through the bag of panties that she had stuffed into her purse and he had confiscated. On his desk was a pile of tags she had pulled off and stuck in the fitting room bench's cushion. To his right on the floor was a huge pile of merchandise, mainly underwear, bras, and jewelry.

Okay, she was a thief, but she was distraught. It was her first time. Couldn't we forgive her one mistake?

Max mocked her crying, "Give it up, I don't believe it for a second. Now tell me, are you wearing anything underneath your clothes? You better tell me now."

She snuffled, "No sir, I do not."

I was livid! Of course she wasn't! She was just like me, a nice, hard-working woman. She maybe had fallen on some hard times. Oh, how I was going to give Max a piece of my mind later!

The next day, I knock on Max's door, cracking my knuckles and rolling my shoulders to prepare for battle. He was really going to get it.

He called out. "Come in!"

I walked into the office, shoulders back, icy glare ready, slapped my hands down and leaned over his desk. I asked, in a tone so cold polar bears would run for cover, "So, what happened to that girl?" *You know, the INNOCENT one,* I thought to myself.

He kept working away at his computer, typing in the last of his notes, not glancing up at me. "Oh, yeah, the police frisked her at the station. She was wearing four bras and thirteen pairs of underwear under her clothes."

Ooooo. Never mind.

The Doggie Defense

Not long after that incident, I had another sad awakening. A lovely customer would always shop our evenings right before closing. She drove a BMW, dressed like Heidi Klum, and to top it all off, she always carried a purse with the cutest little Yorkie I have ever seen lodged inside. Yorkie Lady was supremely charming.

We used to have long conversations by the registers while I pet the little dog's fluffy ears. This went on for maybe a year. After a few weeks I noticed she wasn't coming in anymore. We were in a meeting in the office when I mentioned offhandedly, "I haven't seen the Yorkie lady in a while."

My boss and my coworker looked at each other and cracked up.

"What? What's so funny?" I demanded.

"Are you serious?" asked my boss. "LP got her weeks ago. She's been stealing us blind for months."

My jaw dropped. "What?!" I squawked. "No way!"

"Yes way," my boss responded. "Her purse had a false bottom. She was stealing clothes and stuffing them under the dog. He was her cover."

I'd been betrayed by a Yorkie. I was heartbroken.

Even though I am immune now to caring about thieves, my part-timers love the thrill of the chase. It breaks up the monotony of folding and picking stuff up off the floor. A few times a day I have to discourage an employee from stalking a sketchy customer and mumbling suspicions into the walkie-talkie. Magnum P.I., retail-style.

An example of an associate who took Store Law into her own hands was Michelle. A customer would come back to the counter with a non-receipted return, say a set of expensive sheets. Now, whenever you scan a non-receipted return, the price comes up automatically, and it usually is whatever the item is going for out on the floor. Michelle would look the customer up and down. If the customer looked sketchy, she would type in a lower price.

Customer: I get back $9.99? I think I paid
something like $200 for it.
Michelle: Sorry! That's the price I see!

Let me tell you exactly how many lawsuits we would have had on our hands if she had kept up with this. I'll tell you. A **lot.**

Do only customers steal, you ask? Let's not be silly. A loss prevention district manager told me once that with all inventory shrink, 20% is from general mistakes and missed cataloging,

40% is from outside theft, and 40% is from internal theft. 40% of loss is from employees stealing from us! That means at all times, in all stores, at least one of my associates is stealing money or merchandise right under my nose. How depressing is that?

Speaking of which...

The LP Plot

Our LP officers had been stalking our shoe supervisor for almost eleven months. During that time, they estimated he stole almost $6,000 worth of gift cards, in-store credits, and of course shoes. They also suspected he was part of a small local crime ring. Oftentimes, the officer would see the scurvy shoe sup talking to a notorious non-receipted returner, directly before or after aforementioned notorious returns. The shoe sup (let's call him Sketcher! Get it? Sketchy? And Skechers is a shoe brand? Hahaha, I crack myself up) was giving the criminals the heads-up on any manager on duty.

So needless to say, the LP officers were fed up with Sketcher, but they *could not catch him in the act!* He was too crafty and sneaky. They would see him take a pair of shoes to the back room, but never see him actually take them out of the store. He was seen talking to the criminals, but never exchanging hands with them. They were certain he was pocketing gift cards, but simply could not prove it.

Thus, our LP sups, Cagney and Lacey, hatched their master plot. They set up ceiling cameras in a careful half-moon around a corner aisle of the shoe floor pad. The store manager fixed Sketcher's schedule so he came in a closing shift on a quiet Tuesday. Before Sketcher arrived to clock in, Cagney and Lacey placed an unused $100 gift card on the floor in their secluded aisle. They then proceeded to cover the gift card by tossing fifty plus shoeboxes over it in a haphazard, mishmash, higgledy-piggledy heap. Tissue and shoelaces flew everywhere! It was the LP version of the Princess and the Pea, a.k.a the Big Fat Mess and the Tiny Gift Card.

Cagney and Lacey then parked themselves in the isolated LP office, hulking over their camera screens and waiting impatiently for Sketcher to take the bait. Sketcher, unaware, went about his business, greeting customers, organizing displays, and whistling to himself. The clock ticked on, and the fearless detective duo grew more and more impatient. Sketcher ignored the Big Fat Mess and worked on other projects until almost 9 PM, an hour before closing, when he then decided to take a break. At this point Cagney was tearing her hair out and Lacey was screaming at the screen. "Just steal the gift card. STEAL IT!!!"

While Sketcher was on his break, Ned, the manager on duty, was doing part of his final walk-through. He glanced to his right while passing Shoes and stopped dead in his tracks. What a horrific mess! Being the good manager he was, he decided to help and clean it up. As he started repacking shoeboxes, Cagney and Lacey trampled each other trying to get out the Loss Prevention office door. They shoved back and forth, tripping over each other's feet as Lacey came close to a nosedive on the carpet. Ned glanced up to see two hysterical, screeching LP officers barging down the shoe aisle.

"No, Ned!" Lacey yowled, her voice as screechy as a tea kettle, "Put down that shoe box!"

Terrified, Ned dropped the boxes and put his hands in the air. "I'm sorry! I'm...sorry?"

He had never had such an intense reaction to store recovery before.

Once apprised of the plan, Ned followed the officers and they all holed back up in the office. And of course, you know the rest. Sketchers stole the gift card right in front of their noses and was terminated the next day.

Just kidding! Of course he didn't take the card. It turned out Cagney and Lacey had wasted almost eight hours on the Big Fat Mess plot, almost giving Ned a heart murmur in the process. Sketcher continued to thwart the LP plots for another three months.

What did we finally fire him on, you ask? Theft? Coercion? Fraud?

Attendance.

His attendance had gotten above the limit, so we were able to terminate him. I'm sure he was heartbroken when he lost his livelihood. His only consolation would be the thousands of dollars he stole, and lots and lots and lots of free shoes.

What You Seize is What You Get

Agnes was an 83-year old woman we hired during the holidays. She wasn't the fastest worker, but she charmed customers to the hilt and was one of the top credit-getters in the store. One day Agnes was working the jewelry counter, and a huge bodybuilder dude came up to the display case.

"Um, yeah," he mumbled, "Can I see these sterling silver chains?"

Sweet and eager to help, Agnes opened up the case, "Which one were you looking for, sir?"

"That one." He pointed to a slender chain on the far side of the case. Agnes tried to reach it but couldn't. Inspired, she turned the open case to the guy, exposing about seventy silver chains to him. "Why don't you pick out which one you are looking at?"

The guy grinned. He reached into the case, grabbed *all* the silver chains, and took off running towards the door. Agnes stood there, watching after him in shock. And kept standing there. For about five minutes.

We had this all on video. Agnes' expression made the loss of fifteen hundred dollars' worth of merchandise just about worth it.

Palm d'Store

Another ingenious plot I witnessed happened on a busy Saturday afternoon at our jewelry counter. A pretty young blonde woman politely asked our jewelry associate to look at a pair of diamond studs. Happily, the associate complied. The diamonds were princess cut, single-carat studs, and one of the most expensive things we sell.

The woman asked for a mirror and tried on the earrings, turning her head this way and that to examine the sparkle. The associate would not leave the customer's side, because she had been responsibly trained to never let expensive merchandise out of her sight. The customer took out the earrings and slid them across the counter. "I'll have to talk to my boyfriend. I'm really interested. I'll be back!" She told the associate cheerfully. The associate acknowledged her with a wave and industriously locked up the diamonds into the case.

A few hours later, I received a frantic phone call from the District Manager of Loss Prevention (DMLP) as I was finishing putting an outfit on a mannequin.

"Macy!" she snapped tersely, "I need you to check all your diamond studs. Use the diamond tester."

Perturbed, I agreed. "Do it now. I'll hold." The DMLP said.

Diamond testers are a tool all jewelry counters have. The fact is that no one, not even professionals, can tell the difference between a diamond or a good-looking cubic zirconia without this tool. The only other test is scratching the stone, as CZs will scratch and diamonds will not. The diamond tester looks like a remote control with a small cone and needle sticking out at the end. You press the needle to the diamond and get a happy beep and a green light next to "Diamond" if the diamond is legit. If the diamond is not legit you get an unhappy buzzer and a red light.

I methodically went through all the studs, receiving happy green beeps on each, until I came to the single carats the customer had been shown earlier. There I received a very unhappy red buzzer. I tested again and again, and got the same bad news. I quickly picked up the phone where the DMLP was on hold.

"They aren't diamonds. How can that be?" I asked, picking up the stones and examining them in the light.

It turns out, when Blondie was trying on the studs, she had a pair of cubic zirconia studs in her right hand. After she tried on the studs and held them to her ears, she was switching them in her hands carefully. She slid the fake studs across the counter to my trusting associate, and walked perkily out the door with $7,000 worth of diamond studs palmed in her left hand.

Spill It

A delightful couple walked the jewelry counter, holding hands and looking deeply in love. The man told our jewelry associate they were engaged and getting married in the fall. The man had a Super Gulp cup from 7-11 in his other hand, which holds like nine thousand ounces of soda or something. They requested to see a diamond ring, and the associate unlocked the case, found it, and gingerly held it out to them. The man held it up and examined in the light, then turned to show it to his fiancée. As he did so, he "accidentally" caught his elbow on the cup and spilled soda all over the counter, where it dripped into the cracks and on to some merchandise.

The associate gasped and instinctively turned over her shoulder to grab some paper towels from the counter. When she turned back the couple was gone, diamond ring in hand.

Smooth.

As you can tell, thieves are brazen. I have seen a customer walk in, wave at me cheerfully, head to the Young Men's department, fill his arms full of Levis denim (each pair worth 50 bucks or more), and stride right back out the door, past the registers, alarms blaring, giving me another cheerful wave as he left. I watched him leave in shock. You have to admire that kind of moxie.

Criminals can also be extremely clever. They come up with things that I can't after years of schooling and higher education. If the smart retail thief put his mind to a worldwide problem instead of selling Levis on the black market, he could eradicate malaria.

For example, we have a special store program where a customer earns coupons for every certain amount of money she spends. The incentive is to get the people to spend more at a later time. A sophisticated crime ring in the Northwest figured out that when you return the merchandise and ask for in-store credit, you get to keep the coupons. With this in mind, they started a complicated store–by–store elimination where they purchased $1,000 worth of merchandise in one store, got the coupon, return the thousand dollars worth of merchandise to another store, kept the coupons, then used the in-store credit in the next store to earn more coupons! It was a never-ending cycle, and it was years before our company caught on. We lost thousands of dollars because of this fraud, but when I found out all I could do was marvel at their ingenuity. Let's elect these people to Congress and have them solve the national debt problem! Sure, they may steal the podium out from under the Speaker of the House, but won't it be worth it?

As you can tell, I have the utmost respect for our LP team.[36] But in fact, I saw a sign in a small retail store that I think is probably just as effective as anything our LP team has ever done.

Hahahahahahahahhaahhahahahahhahahahhahahhahha hahahahahaahahahhahahahahhahahah!

I think a sad puppy face is more effective than any hard tags LP makes us put on Junior panties. Sad puppy faces makes criminals think twice. I think that should be in all cop handbooks.

So in a brief chapter summary - you should never steal. Bad, bad you, for even THINKING about it. Stealing is a terrible thing!

But if you do, you won't get caught. Just make sure you keep all your bras on.

Chapter 14

Letters From A Shrew

"I personally think we developed language because of our deep need to complain."

-Lily Tomlin

If you are really angry with a store, the best way to hit 'em hard it is to send a letter to Corporate. You can call the store itself, but our upper management team consists of maybe four people, and we've all got each other's backs. If you call to complain about a rude assistant manager named Bill, I will sympathetically commiserate with you and promised to follow up with him. Then I *will* follow up with Bill about it, but I will do it while we're at happy hour at Applebee's, making fun of you over potato twisters.

An e-mail (or even better, a physical letter) to Corporate, however, gets filtered through a chain of command. It starts with the Corporate complaint team, who figures out the appropriate store, sends it to the territory manager, who sends it to the DM, who sends it to your store manager with the insistence that you follow-up or you will be in big trubz.

I have been in charge of many of these e-mails, and I sent copies to my home email just for this book. For your reading pleasure, I am pleased to present to you an actual Letter From a Shrew.

Dear _____ -37

On the morning of January 12 I visited your store with my husband to buy him khakis. I have visited your stores in the past and I must say that this was the worst experience I've ever had. When we first entered no one greeted us at the door. We expect as paying customers to always be greeted, no matter the time of day. We went to the pants aisle and found that some of the D3s had been mixed with the D4s. You can imagine how we felt!

---

[37] Much as I love me a good lawsuit, I will not be mentioning my store's name.

How could anyone possibly find what they're looking for when pants are mixed?

When we went to the cashier, the pants we found didn't match the price on the sign. Although the cashier fixed it right away it is still unbelievable that the prices don't match. It is misleading, and I have half a mind to report you to the government. My brother is a lawyer and he says we have a real case.

I request a reply. I spent over $50 in your store in the last six months, but if I am not compensated for the inconvenience of my last visit I will be spending my money elsewhere.

Insincerely,

Mrs. Nasty Shrew

We deal with letters like this on a regular basis. Below it there is usually a short note from the DM saying, "You need to reply in the next 24 hours or I'm throwing you all in the streets." Okay, it doesn't actually say that, but I know my DM would write that if he could. So I have to write back to Mrs. N. Shrew, who really didn't have that bad of an experience. No greeting? Sorry, but our cashiers are crazy busy and we don't have Walmart greeters at the door. Mixed-up pants? D3s and D4s look identical to each other, except one is pleated and one is flat. It's almost impossible to keep them separated unless we had a Dockers sorting crew. Prices didn't match? You got the price you wanted. So what, exactly, is your problem, Mrs. Shrew? Why don't you go home and cook up some larvae for Mr. Shrew's dinner?

My favorite letters are the ones that are clearly written by illiterate bonobos, or so it would seem. These letters are misspelled, mistyped, and grammatically incorrect. I am surprised they figured out how to use email, what with their little prehensile hands and all.

Example:

To the companie- i am writing because you're companie gave me the worst custommer servece ever!!! i was looking for knew skinie jeans and they sold out and then were sold out agin the next day!! i know my buisines doesnt mattter to you or you wuld get the jeans in. im not shopping their agin!! -janice d.

I struggled writing back to these types of letters. *To the custommer, were soo sorrie!* My technique is generally to write the most slavishingly boot-licking wallowing obsequious beg-your-forgiveness letter I can muster up. Here is a true email I wrote:

Dear Mrs. ____-

I cannot apologize enough for the terrible service you received on _____ in our store. The way you were treated was completely unacceptable. Please rest assured I will follow-up with the associate responsible for this situation. He was way out of line with his comment that you "look in another store" for the item you wanted since we were out of stock. He should have tried harder to make that item appear for you in our store.

Trust me when I tell you that you are a deeply valued customer. We appreciate your business and realize you could be shopping elsewhere. Please accept our deepest and most sincere apologies as well as this 20% off coupon. I look forward to the day we can serve you again! We simply couldn't be the company we are today without wonderful customers like you and I want to thank you for your patronage.

Again, we are just so, so, so, so very sorry, and hope so very much you give us another chance! Can I apologize again? We're so sorry!

Sincerely,

Macy May Marcus, ASM

My DM loved this letter. He clearly didn't see it for what it was - a big fat sarcastic up-yours to the lady. I write these letters dripping in sarcasm, but customers never see it. They truly believe they are entitled to boot-licking. I see this all the time on the sales floor when I am sarcastically nice. Only one woman has ever called me on it, and that was only for a moment. I said, "Oh my God, I am SO sorry there's a tear in your shoe! That's so awful! Whatever are we going to do??" She peered at me and said, "Are you making fun of me?" In the same tone, I said, "Oh, NO! Certainly not! I would never do that! This tear is just so TERRIBLE!" Warily she said, "Yes, this tear shouldn't have happened." I said, "No, I TOTALLY agree!" And just like that she was satisfied again. It just goes to show how self-satisfied people are.

There are countless more emails, but there are too many to put in this book. Let me sum the rest of them up for you.

Dear _____ –

Blah-blah-blah worst customer service ever blah blah blah I've been shopping there for years blah blah blah I couldn't find what I was looking for blah blah blah why isn't customer service in the front of the store you should fix that I hate walking more than ten feet blah blah blah if you don't get me a rain check on that patio umbrella I'm going to firebomb the store blah blah blah why don't you have a larger selection of Justin Bieber T-shirts blah blah blah I'm never going to shop there again unless you send me a $50 gift card blah blah blah I also want a 15% off coupon blah blah blah and a free Bieber t-shirt blah blah blah but not the yellow one, only the green one blah blah blah you really need more Bieber t-shirts blah blah blah and I hate you!

Sincerely,

A Shrew[38]

---

[38] Or if it's from a teenager, it's a shrewlet. This book came close to being named Macy and the Shrewlets. Maybe for the sequel.

Obnoxious as the letters are, they get results. To ~~keep from getting fired~~ keep our customers happy, we give out coupons, honor prices, promise dollars off, and pretty much do whatever the customer wants to bring them back to the store. The more high-maintenance you are as a Shrew, the more free stuff you get.

This is my retail motto:

Give Them What They Want So They Go Away.

I live by this motto. I am not paid enough to save the company money. If it requires that I lie to you to give you the answer that you want so you go away, I will do it. If I'm wrong, oh well. We have an excellent return policy!

I have learned this the hard way. I see this in all my new associates. When they begin, they are not yet willing to let the Shrews get away with murder. When customers insist on another 30% off discount because of a dented package, my little newbies try to stand up for the store. In quavering voices, they say, "No, I'm sorry, I saw your child fling the package out of your cart at your other child's head. That's why it is dented."

Then I come up to them, pat their sweet naive heads gently, and say, "Don't fight it, kiddo. Give them the 30% off."

The reason I do this is because this is what Corporate wants. Corporate lives in terrifying fear of alienating a single customer and a single wallet, therefore, they give customers what they want when they want it. My harsh wake-up call on this came about two months into my training. An obese woman who looked like she ate a cupcake shop waddled into luggage and pressed the callbox button for help. Ten minutes later I found her squatting over a 5-piece set of luggage. "Hello!" I said cheerily (this was at the beginning of my retail career, when I still had cheer). "How can I help you?"

"Oh, yes," she said, straightening up, "I had a question about this sign. It says Buy One Get One Free. Does that include both brands?"

I examined the sign carefully. In print on the bottom it clearly stated that the brand she was looking at was the only one excluded. I pointed this out to her.

"Oh darn," she said, sorrowfully. "Well, I guess that's pretty clear."

She waddled off, and I didn't give the matter a second thought until our store received an angry email from corporate. Apparently the woman, who to my surprise was a Secret Shrew, had written the company and voiced her unhappiness about the brand being excluded and the sign being unclear. Corporate demanded that we 1.) Write a letter of apology to the woman, 2.) Invite her back to the store with a 30% off coupon for future purchases, and 3.) GIVE HER A FREE SET OF THE 300 DOLLAR LUGGAGE!

I was blown away. We had had a clear conversation about the sign, she seemed amicable and in agreement, or so I thought. That is when I learned that corporate will give customers what they want, when they want it, and I had better get on board.

The typical Shrew is a middle-aged woman.[39] She has shopped at your store for years, which is surprising considering how much she hates everything about your store. One Shrew can write more angry letters and be upset about more things in one day than your

[39] Or man. HeShrews can be as nasty as SheShrews.

average shopper can be in a year. Shrews demand excellent customer service at all times and make no concessions for any extenuating circumstances, such as time of day, time of year, or business level. Shrews will watch your cashier try to juggle three customers at once and then write a letter saying she hadn't been offered a cart. Shrews have obviously never worked retail, because they are shocked when the Toys aisle is a mess as they watch unattended children throw Barbies at each other across the aisles. Shrews are the peak of the Low Spender/High Suffer customers. They will demand your undivided attention for forty-five minutes to help them pick out a pair of five-dollar earrings. And then they will write a nasty letter to Corporate saying that you did not know the metal compound formula of the metal in the earrings like you should have.

Shrews get what they want, and you had better accept it. Fighting it is futile. Contrary to Shakespeare's opinion, you will not tame any Shrew. Copy and paste my ingratiating letter as your e-mail reply to a Shrew Letter and get your free $300 luggage set ready. The only way to take solace is to think about how unhappy the Shrews are on a daily basis, as it is exhausting to be annoyed with everything all the time. If you are not a Shrew, then be grateful. You may not be receiving free items, but you will be a happier person for it. And you will save a fortune on postage.

Chapter 15

Vendor Vexations

"I never go straight to the point if I can go the most difficult way. Why be simple when you can be complicated?"

-Kristin Scott Thomas

There is one phrase I dread even more than, "A customer wants to speak to a manager."

This phrase is, "The Girl's Hair Accessories lady wants to see a manager."

I am *terrified* of the Girl's Hair Accessories vendor. Doris is about sixty years old and looks like an aging hippie, but not the peace-love-kindness kind. She wears flowing dresses printed with whacked-out butterflies and flowers, and her hair is always loose and crazy around her shoulders, streaked with grey. When she gets upset (which is often) she shakes her head like a soggy dog, frizzing out her hair even more.

The Girl's Hair Accessories Lady gets VERY ANGRY that our store does not spend sufficient girl's hair accessories recovery time. Girl's Hair Accessories is approximately 1/1,000,000th of my business. If you put all the profits from Girl's Hair Accessories sales, combined from all stores, across the entire country, it may approximate the profits from the sale of one vacuum cleaner.

REGARDLESS, Girl's Hair Accessories requires the UTMOST CARE and DETAIL! According to Doris, I should hire a FULL-TIME Girl's Hair Accessories detailer!

Then we have the Bra Lady. We ADORE the Bra Lady. Candy the Bra Lady comes in and organizes all our bras, by color, style, and type of bra strap. She never complains, never demands, and when she leaves our bra section looks like it was touched by angels. Until the customers get to it.

Vendors are the deputies of large-name brands who go from department store to department store to make sure their brands are being represented correctly, look nice, and are sell-able. Some examples are Levi's, Gold Toe Socks, Maidenform, and Dockers. These brands are in all different types of department stores, each with different organizations and emphasis. The vendors come to the stores periodically, sign in at Customer Service, and evaluate their displays. Then, depending on their personalities, they clean up (good vendor!) or try to make **me** clean up (bad vendor!)

Vendors range from the good ones like Candy to the evil ones like Doris. Regardless, there is one type of vendor I like - the kind that leaves me alone. Vendors who try to engage me in a conversation about the correct angle of their pashmina fixture are in for a rude awakening. I have no time for you. None. You are honestly lucky that your pashminas have made it to the floor at all. Usually my Accessories associate calls out for a week at a time, and I have to make my ad set guys put out your pashminas. The men obviously are very familiar with the product and your planograms and your brand, considering they begin their merchandising like this: "So, what's a pashmina?"

Vendors use the same thing we do: a blueprint called planograms, plano-grams, plan-o-grams, schematics and POGs. Almost all stores use these to bring uniformity to visual displays. Planograms have all the information you need to put out product correctly, such as the color order, number of items to put out, and how to dress the mannequins.

However, planograms are created by corporate college graduates with a LOT of time on their hands. They like to give store associates incredibly detailed planograms because they think we have the time to follow them. (See Chapter 4: The Corporate Problem) Hah. Foolish little graduates. Planograms are utilized as such:

Planogram- How It Is Meant to Be Used:

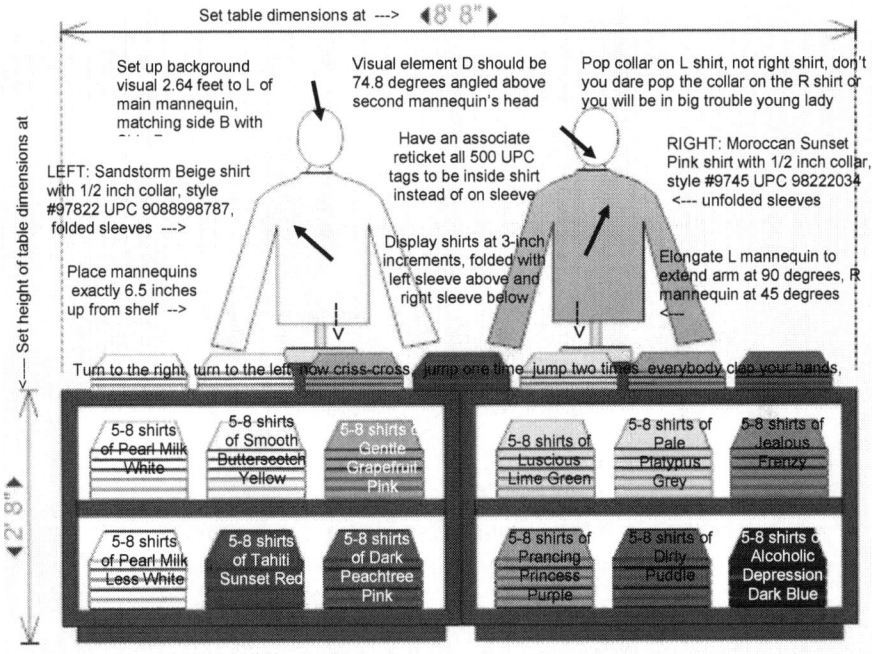

Set table dimensions at ---> ◀8' 8"▶

Set height of table dimensions at ---

◀2' 8"▶

Set up background visual 2.64 feet to L of main mannequin, matching side B with

Visual element D should be 74.8 degrees angled above second mannequin's head

Pop collar on L shirt, not right shirt, don't you dare pop the collar on the R shirt or you will be in big trouble young lady

LEFT: Sandstorm Beige shirt with 1/2 inch collar, style #97822 UPC 9088998787, folded sleeves --->

Have an associate reticket all 500 UPC tags to be inside shirt instead of on sleeve

RIGHT: Moroccan Sunset Pink shirt with 1/2 inch collar, style #9745 UPC 98222034

<--- unfolded sleeves

Place mannequins exactly 6.5 inches up from shelf -->

Display shirts at 3-inch increments, folded with left sleeve above and right sleeve below

Elongate L mannequin to extend arm at 90 degrees, R mannequin at 45 degrees

Turn to the right, turn to the left, now criss-cross, jump one time, jump two times, everybody clap your hands,

5-8 shirts of Pearl Milk White

5-8 shirts of Smooth Butterscotch Yellow

5-8 shirts of Gentle Grapefruit Pink

5-8 shirts of Luscious Lime Green

5-8 shirts of Pale Platypus Grey

5-8 shirts of Jealous Franzy

5-8 shirts of Pearl Milk Less White

5-8 shirts of Tahiti Sunset Red

5-8 shirts of Dark Peachtree Pink

5-8 shirts of Prancing Princess Purple

5-8 shirts of Dirty Puddle

5-8 shirts of Alcoholic Depression Dark Blue

Planogram - How It Is Actually Used:

On a truck day we get thousands of pieces of merchandise. We get collections in belts, underwear, and socks in Men's Basics, sets of flatware in Home, and millions and millions of flip-flops in Accessories. **Every one of these has a planogram.** We are meant to have trucks done in one day. Therefore, you sweet little college graduate with a BA in English who is writing these planos at Corporate, your planograms are not going to be followed to the letter. They actually aren't going to be followed at all. Your time would be better spent figuring out new and sophisticated ways to raise my salary.

While corporate peons make the planos, it's the vendors who check to make sure they are implemented. If they are vendors like Candy, they ask me, "Is the new grey fixture in the back? I'll bring it out, put it together, and set the new planogram of Maidenform bras out for you." Then I say, "I love you, Candy!" If they are vendors like Doris, they say, "Macy, the plano says the pink scrunchies go to the LEFT of the blue scrunchies!" Then I say, "I have a phone call in the back I need to take, Doris!"

When I first started retail, I was very concerned about the vendors' needs. The first month I started working - this is true– I spent two hours listening to the Carter's lady explained to me how to colorize and organize baby socks. I had a notebook out and was taking notes, drawing little baby socks in minute detail. The vendor, of course, was delighted to have the undivided attention of a manager, since she was ignored in every other store by more seasoned retail veterans. When I got back to the office, my boss asked where I'd been. When I told him, he laughed so loud the administrative assistant peeked in to see what was the matter. "Macy," he said, rubbing his teary eyes, "Let me give you a rule of retail. Let the vendors do their job, and you do yours. Your job description does not have baby socks anywhere in it."

I took those words to heart. So this message is to Doris - your scrunchies will always remain out of order, as long as I manage my department. My job description says nothing about scrunchies. But I'm pretty sure yours does. So take a hint from Candy and organize on your own.

And in return, maybe I'll try to keep your Girl's Hair Accessories off the floor. Maybe I'll try.

Chapter 16

How To Get What You Want from Retailers, or, Be Nice and Ask Twice

"It is nice to be important, but it's more important to be nice."

-John Templeton

There are 5 rules to getting what you want from burnt-out, minimum-wage paid, surly, apathetic retail associates.

1.) Be Nice

I cannot say this enough. Be nice be nice be nice be nice be nice be <u>NICE!</u> Being nasty really *will* get you far, don't get me wrong. You already know that my motto with difficult customers is Give Them What They Want So They Go Away. Angry customers will make me scramble to make them happy, but there is a limit. I have some control in my store (surprisingly) and I can put the brakes on some things if you push me too far. I can pretend to search online for you and then lie about what inventory other stores have, just to punish you for being a jerk. So don't go the nasty route.

It's the nice ones that I will do anything for. I will call other stores for you. I will research clearance items that are no longer on the floor. I will give you the extra "friends and family" discount. I will track down your one-of-a-kind pink purse to the outer treks of the universe. But only after you...

2.) Ask Twice

The first question is a warm-up. I will listlessly look through the racks for your size, but I don't care yet. It's the second (nice) query that will actually get me to care and realize you will not be sent away. I will always palm off a customer with some generic phrases about how, "It's not in stock yet," or "Maybe on the next truck," if I can get away with it. My day is too busy to give the utmost care to every customer. But if you ask me twice (nicely) I will take you more seriously and start putting more effort into the search.

If I still can't get it, you need to...

3.) Be Persistent

Be *nicely* persistent. If you smile and asked me sweetly to check just one more time, I will. As I mentioned before, my store motto is to give customers what they want so they go away and leave me alone. But always reference rule number 1– be nice!

If you demand petulantly that I check the stockroom when I absolutely, positively *know* we are out of the item, I will be irritated. I will go to the back docilely, then I will proceed to sit on a stockroom bench, cool my heels, and check my watch until enough time has passed that I can come out and tell you one more time– we *do not have the item*. One time, I was so mad at a customer who insisted I check the back twice, when she demanded I look for the second time, I went into the stock room, snuck into the break room through the back door, and proceeded to take my break. Fifteen minutes later, I strolled up to her and gushed, " Oh, I checked absolutely everywhere! That's why it took so long! Sorry, still don't have it." My pretend checking had consisted of a cup of coffee, a granola bar, and my feet propped up.

If there's no progress in finding your item, you should...

4.) Bribe Me

Bribe me with offers of compliments to my district manager. Not my store manager - he already knows me. And he better already think that I am amazing. My DM is the big dawg. Ask for the DM's e-mail or phone number, or a corporate line you can call. This goes through the higher powers-that-be and reflects very well on me. I am going to step it up if you make it worth my while.

After you've sweet-talked me and had no success, your next option is to...

5.) Ask More Than One Associate

Waiters get very annoyed by this, because when customers ask three different waiters for a side of ranch dressing, they end up with three sides of ranch dressing that they of course don't finish. However, it is effective in retail. We have a whole range of experience in our store. You don't know if the person you spoke to really knows what they're talking about. I've had new associates intentionally lie to customers because they didn't want to seem ignorant. Or if they aren't intentionally lying, they are doing so unintentionally. "Oh, no, we're out of those dog beds," they tell a customer, because they truly don't know we have hundreds more moldering in the back.

So it is best to ask all sorts of people. Ask the checker, ask the customer service person, ask the floor people. Or ask an employee to speak to the manager, but make this your final step, because as I mentioned before, I hate being pulled from projects and will transfer my hate onto you when I meet you. But as a rule managers generally know the most (unless the manager is my recent boss- see Chapter 6).

One adorable lady shopping in my store exemplified these steps in their entirety. Let's call her Nana. Nana was petite, curly-haired and about a hundred years old. She was looking for some stuffed ducks that we had sold months ago to buy for her grandkids. All the stores had been out for a long, long while, and they were discontinued so we wouldn't be getting any more in. Nana asked three people on the floor before she got to me, and each had unequivocally told her we were totally out.

Finally, she found me in the kids section and pounced.

She asked me, sweet as sugar, displaying a white and yellow fluffy duck in her hand, "Can you see if you have any more of these ducks? I have seven grandchildren, and I really want them all to have one."

I knew we were out and prepared to let her down gently. "I'm so sorry, those were last season, and I know we are out." I said.

She smiled, looking like an angelic Bea Arthur, "Is there any chance you can check for me, please? My grandkids would *so* love them."

I sighed and got out my checking device, and proceeded scrolling through the stores. "Sorry, this store is out...and this one...and this one....and there are none online...." I went through about ten stores.

"I'm sorry, ma'am, there are none in this region at all." I told her, preparing to walk away.

With a gentle touch she grasped my forearm, keeping me in place. "You are such a dear for doing this for me. Can you check a few more stores? And I must tell your manager how delightful you are. Who do I email so I can sing your praises?" She beamed at me, somehow projecting this warm, positive feeling that I was simply the most capable employee that ever walked this earth.

All of a sudden I was more motivated on my duck hunt. "Okay, I'm still looking..." I went through an additional TWENTY stores' listing and found ONE store in Reno that had a few ducks left. "I'll give them a call!" I said jubilantly.

I rang the store up, and inquired about the ducks. They said they had them, and I begged for a transfer. We rarely do transfers because they are time-consuming and a big hassle, but I was pretty much in love with Nana at this point, and by God her grandkids were going to get some stuffed ducks! After much negotiation, the store agreed to send them, and Nana went home happy, after giving me a huge hug and a piece of old candy from her purse. Trust me, there was *no way* I would have done 1/10th of that amount of work for a nasty customer or a customer who didn't ask twice.

The morale of the story is follow these easy five steps, and you will get your stuffed ducks!

Why I Do It: The 5 Reasons This Snarky Girl Sticks With Retail

So you have just read hundreds of pages about how much I hate fitting rooms, the return system, loss prevention, the holidays, price changes, registers, my employees, and all of my whiny, irksome, demanding, and unhinged customers.

And your question is now- *so why do you do it???*

If I despise retail so much, why do I stick with it? Why do I get up every morning (or afternoon) and make my way to my perpetually fluorescent-lit building? Why do I struggle through snowstorms and power outages to keep the doors open for customers? Why do I do this job?

I have five reasons.

1.) I always have a good story.

If I come home from work and I don't have a crazy consumer story, I consider the day a loss. Working with the public is an experience like none other. I see hundreds of people a day, and a great majority of them are rude, clueless, and socially impaired. I have been compiling these stories for the past seven years. I come home from work and jot down the crazy customer I had for the day in my journals. My friends love inviting me to parties because I regale them with stories, and every story is 100% true! Actuaries just don't get the same level of insanity on a daily basis. Poor guys. There will be no *Rant Of An Actuary* book in production anytime soon.

2.) I am never bored.

A typical day in retail is atypical. No two days are the same - ever. Here is one day in the life of a retail manager.

8:00am: Clock in.

8:01am: Pick up walkie-talkie and scanner, put on name tag.

8:05am: Check email.

8:06am: Be interrupted from email over the walkie-talkie from a confused register associate about how to ring up a two-for-one item.

8:09 am: Check email.

8:11am: Be interrupted from email by the fire alarm guys, who need to get roof access.

8:15am: Climb ladder to roof to open the door. Watch fire alarm guys climb up. Warn fire alarm guys not to let customers on roof, even though should probably be obvious.

8:18am: Check email.

8:21am: Be interrupted from email by admin, who wants to know what time to schedule team to reorganize beauty department.

8:26am: Check email.

8:27am: Be interrupted from email by employee on phone alerting me that Girl's Hair Accessories lady is in the building. Hide in closed-door office to avoid Girl's Hair Accessories lady.

8:38am: Check email.

8:39am: Be interrupted from email by call from customer service employee, informing that the gift registry is down.

8:41am: Give up on email.

8:45am: Try to repair gift registry. Accidentally pull registry cords out of the wall. Try to put cords back. Fail.

9:12 am: Call help desk on getting gift registry repaired.

9:17am: Be hung up on by help desk.

9:22am: Call back help desk. Threaten help desk with bodily harm if help desk does not get repair guy out today.

9:37am: Begin project to clean up women's flip-flops.

9:38am: Be called by employee who says fire alarm guys have let a customer on the roof.

9:45am: Avoid major lawsuit by talking customer into coming down the ladder off the roof.

10:30am: Begin project to clean up women's flip-flops.

10:31am: Be interrupted from project by housekeeping, who needs the garbage compactor door unlocked.

10:48am: Begin project to clean up women's flip-flops.

10:49am: Be interrupted from project by overhead screeching noise as sound system breaks down.

10:55am: Call help desk and request assistance on sound system.

10:57am: Be hung up on by help desk.

10:59am: Call back help desk and use colorful language describing exactly what will do to help desk person unless sound system guy comes to repair sound system.

11:15am: Consider break.

11:16am: Be interrupted from consideration of break by phone call from angry customer. Listen to twenty-minute tirade against lack of bathrobes in store. Express deep sympathy and regret over lack of bathrobes and promise restitution.

11:19am: Consider break.

11:20am: Be interrupted from consideration of break by change request from registers.

11:25am: Give change to cashier.

11:26 am: Consider break.

11:27am: Be interrupted from consideration of break by cashier claiming she wanted pennies, not quarters. Return to register. Explain to cashier she should write in the pennies line, not the quarters line, in order to receive pennies. Re-do change request.

11:32am: Consider break.

11:33am: Preemptively give up on concept of break.

11:34am: Return to project to clean up women's flip-flops.

11:35am: Be interrupted by lost child crying and wandering through the purse department.

11:36am: Attempt to find child's parents. Hold child's hand. Immediately regret holding child's hand, as observe chocolate smears transferred to palm.

11:45am: Find child's mother. Mother confused as to why child is unattended in purse department, when she clearly left child unattended in the *toys* department.

11:58pm: Give up on project to clean up women's flip-flops.

12:00pm: Lunch.

12:01pm: Interrupted from lunch by angry customer who wants the senior discount, even though technically forty-year-olds are not seniors. Give senior discount.

12:16pm: Lunch.

12:17pm: Interrupted from lunch by loss prevention manager requesting assistance in apprehending meth addict, who is systemically tearing open all video game packages and shouting at customers walking by.

12:39pm: Give statement to police regarding meth addict's choices of video games and language.

12:55pm: Lunch.

12:56pm: Interrupted from lunch by customer injury. Old man has slipped on tile next to "Caution-Wet Floor Sign".

1:30pm: Fill out accident report.

2:00pm: Call injury hotline. Repeat everything just wrote in accident report.

2:37pm: Lunch

2:38pm: Interrupted from lunch by associate, questioning why hours were cut. Explain to associate that he does not show up to work, and when he does show up, he does a bad job. Explain how attendance and doing work relate to earning money.

2:49pm: Give up on lunch.

2:55pm: Receive angry phone call from district manager demanding to know why sales are so bad. Go to floor and tell employees to increase sales. Observe employees not care.

3:28pm: Have sit-down with boss on beauty project. Agree with boss on everything.

3:45pm: Continue plan on beauty project. Ignore everything boss recommends.

4:17pm: Encounter crying associate who runs into office, distraught over cheating boyfriend. Console.

5:00pm: Clock out.

5:01pm: Attempt to leave store.

5:02pm: Be interrupted on way out by angry customer over lack of price scanners in store. Point to price scanner two feet away.

5:03pm: Attempt to leave store.

5:04pm: Be interrupted on way out by distressed associate over fitting room situation. Call store-wide fitting room blitz.

5:14pm: Attempt to leave store.

5:15pm: Be interrupted on leaving by fire alarm guys, who need the roof door locked.

5:16pm: Attempt to leave store.

5:32pm: Duck behind fixtures. Do careful ninja customer-avoidance moves, working towards the back of the store. Sneak out back through the freight door.

5:45pm: Check off another successful day in retail.

6:00pm: Write chapter in snarky retail book.

This is of course only an example of a retail day. Most days do not go so smoothly.

3.) I am changing the world - in my own little way.

My store rewards terrible behavior. When you are a jerk, you get what you want. I see this as a growing phenomenon across the country in US businesses, ranging from the airlines to restaurants. The person who throws the biggest temper tantrum gets the biggest rewards. Since we give people what they want when they behave badly, obviously they will continue behaving badly. It's like children! What we need to do is say, "NO! Bad girl! You MAY NOT have a discount! If you keep throwing that tantrum, I am going to take away your credit card! Go to time-out!"

I try to fight this system sometimes by 1.) Not giving grown-up brats what they want, and 2.) Giving the nice customers what they want.

I had one situation when a customer made a non-receipted return. Unfortunately it was worth only 3.99 since it had gone clearance a few weeks ago.

"Oh, shoot." She said. "I paid 19.99 for it." She sighed. "I should have kept the receipt. Okay, I will take the 3.99."

No whining, no hissy fit, no accusations. Complete responsibility for her mistake. So rare!

I thought for a minute - if she had screamed at me, I would give her the 19.99. Why not give it to her because she is NOT screaming at me?

"Let's honor that 19.99 for you, ma'am." I told her.

Her face lit up. "Thank you!"

"No problem!" I said, feeling renewed. I try to reward good customers for being good people. I am helping, in my own way, to save our culture from being a bunch of spoiled brats. One transaction at a time.

4.) I will always have a job.

As long as people need stuff, I am employed. And people will always, always, always need stuff.

An estimated two-thirds of the U.S. gross domestic product (GDP) comes from retail consumption. According to Fortune Magazine's Fortune 500 Companies for 2012, the number two company of all industries, not only in the US, but in the *world*, is a retailer: Walmart.

People love their stuff. Stuff means prosperity, security, wealth, and status. Stuff is reassuring. It's a safety net. We love our stuff so much that we have major television shows dedicated to hoarders. We watch these shows to feel better about ourselves. "Well, I love all my stuff too much to get rid of anything for the past ten years, but look at this woman! At least I don't have fifty years of newspapers and kitty litter in my basement!"

We love to consume. It's a pastime, a recreational activity, a form of therapy. While retail therapy isn't in the DSM-IV psychology manual yet, it may be on its way. So as long as people buy new things, I will never be in the unemployment line. It's nice to have job security. Even if it's not the most glamorous job in the world.

5.) I honestly like people.

I know, I know. It sure doesn't sound like it. But even with the high percentage of nutters who come through my doors, I have an even higher percentage of absolutely darling customers. I have little old ladies who give me a hug after I find them the umbrella they were looking for. I have sweet teenagers who ask my opinion on the prom dresses they are trying on, and who are honestly thrilled when I approve. I have mothers that beam at me when I find them a stroller with a kid's seat, and compliment me on my outfit.

When my associates are having a really rough day, I will pull them together and ask each of them to tell the story of the best customer they ever had. Here are some of those stories:

I helped a lady to her car with a big lawn chair. She thanked me over and over and tried to tip me. When I turned it down, she came in the next day and gave me a plate of cookies she had baked. She said she would always look for me whenever she came in. - Jared

I returned some old items for a customer and fixed some errors that another store had made on her receipt. She said I was the best customer service person she had ever seen, in any company. It made my day. -Kimberly

An old couple was looking for cruise wear. I helped them all around the store and we found them a leisure suit and lots of cruise dresses. They loved me so much, they invited me and my husband out to dinner that weekend. I thought it was a casual thing, but when they told me the address to meet them at, it was a four-star restaurant! Just for helping them find resort wear! -Mandy

A little old lady told me I was working very hard, and gave me a tootsie roll. It was adorable. She said I deserved a reward for my hard work and that she appreciated it. It was the best tootsie roll I ever ate. -Karla

My favorite customer always comes in the evening and gives me a hug every time she sees me. She says I brighten her day. -Clea

I have a regular who has been shopping at my store for the past fifteen years. She always calls ahead to be sure I will be working when she comes in. We talk on the sales floor and she always asks about my kids. I give her fashion advice and she always heads home with a big purchase (and a big commission for me). She's not only a wonderful customer, I consider her a friend. - Shawna

And as for my favorite customer story, I was working the Misses department when a sad-looking woman asked for my help one afternoon. I looked at her and saw black circles under eyes and deeply etched sorrow lines on her face. She told me she was looking for clothes to wear to her mother's funeral, who had passed away the week before. I led her throughout the store, and we picked out clothes together. She didn't want black, because her mother was a cheerful, joyful person, and she wanted to celebrate her. She told me sweet stories about her mom as we wandered the aisles, and we both teared up.

At the end, she touched my arm, looked me in the eyes, and thanked me with a voice tight with emotion. She said, "You have helped me during the toughest time of my life. I will always be grateful."

I will never forget that experience. My job is not glamorous. I do not solve the world's problems. At the end of the day, all I do is sell stuff.

But for one afternoon, I helped someone, and that is of value.

THE END

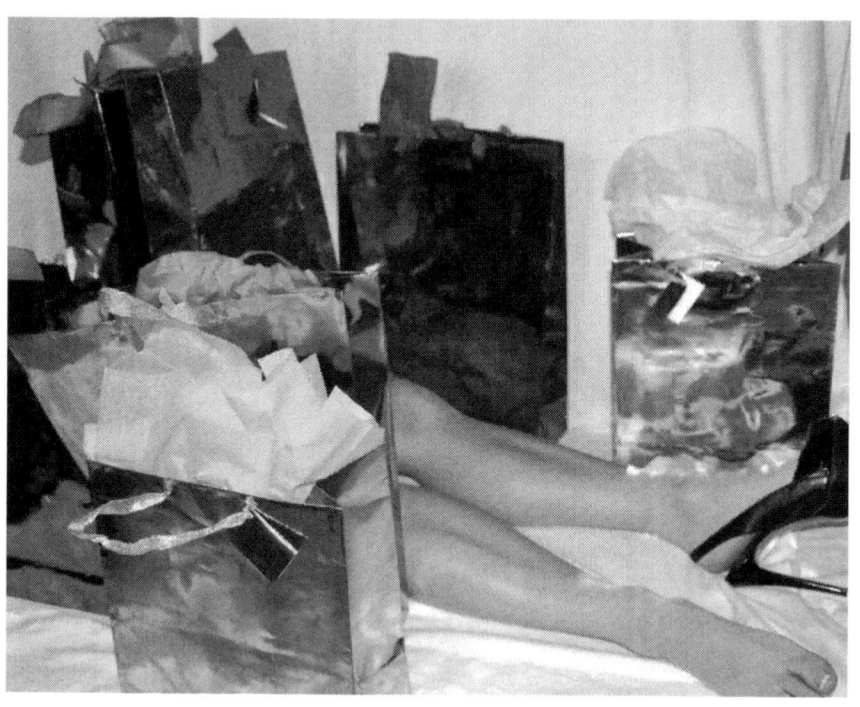

Thank you SO MUCH for purchasing and reading my book!

You are clearly a very savvy reader with an excellent sense of humor. And of course ridiculously good-looking too.

If you could, please take a moment to rate my book on Amazon.

5 Stars would be so rad.

Acknowledgments

First of all, I'd like to thank my stores. Thank you for hiring me and keeping me around for all these years, even though you were unaware I'd write a snarky book about the world of retail. Sorry about that.

To Dave Barry - thanks for being, in my humble opinion, the funniest person in the world. You've inspired both my writing style and my sense of humor. You will always be the equivalent of a Backstreet Boy to me.

Many thanks for the advice of my fellow writer friends - Brandon Wu and Laura Pepper Wu and David C. Dykstra.

To Mark S. Young, thanks for everything - taking me to LoveLine, putting me to work researching your book *The Mirror Effect* with Dr. Drew, and even giving me credit at the end. Your book is a little bit more of a bestseller than mine, but I am returning the favor!

Thank you to the Eddy clan - to Aunt Brenda, for always being the first in line to support me, Uncle Charlie for taking me in that summer, and for all the Eddy siblings - for their help, advice, love, and for being far funnier than I am.

Danny Griffin - thank you for being the best, best, best, best, best boss and for teaching me how a store is actually supposed to run.

Eternal love and gratitude to my Alpha Chi Omegas: Justine Baldacci, Alisha Farnell, Kathleen Heesch, Michelle Conzonire (Michelle #1), and Michelle Crowe (Michelle #2). I didn't know when I walked into our house on Rush Day that I would find my lifelong friends, but wow. Seriously did.

To my baby girl Pacey Grace - you light up my life with your sunny smile. I am grateful for you every day.

And finally, my mom and my husband, I love you both so much. I dedicated this book to you, but what the heck, I'm thanking you in the acknowledgments too. That's how great you are.

References

Chapter 1

1. http://www.mckinseyquarterly.com/Motivating_people_Getting_beyond_money_2460

Chapter 2

1. George F. Dreher, Ronald A. Ash, Priscilla Hancock, December 7, 2006, http://onlinelibrary.wiley.com/doi/10.1111/j.1744-6570.1988.tb02387.x/abstract

2. http://www.management-issues.com/2006/8/24/research/references-resumes-and-interviews-useless-at-predicting-success.asp

3. Betty Lehan Harrigan, Games Mother Never Taught You (New York: Warner Books, 1977) 55.

4. National Retail Federation, *Women in Retail*, Washington DC: were010, http://www.nrf.com/modules.php?name=Pages&sp_id=1247

5. The Fiscal Times, *How Men and Women Differ in the Workplace*, New York: 2012 http://www.thefiscaltimes.com/Articles/2012/05/25/How-Men-and-Women-Differ-in-the-Workplace.aspx#page1

6. Malcolm Gladwell. Blink: The Power of Thinking Without Thinking. Little, Brown and Company, New York: 2005

Chapter 3

1. Ronald E. Milliman, The Journal of MarketingVol. 46, No. 3 (Summer, 1982), pp. 86-91 Published by: American Marketing Association http://www.jstor.org/discover/10.2307/1251706?uid=2129&uid=2&uid=70&uid=4&sid=47698764398957

2. Richard F. Yalch, Eric Spangenberg (1993), "USING STORE MUSIC FOR RETAIL ZONING: A FIELD EXPERIMENT", in Advances in Consumer Research Volume 20, eds. Leigh McAlister and Michael L. Rothschild, Provo, UT : Association for Consumer Research, Pages: 632-636.http://www.acrwebsite.org/volumes/display.asp?id=7531

Chapter 4

1. http://www.dailyfinance.com/2010/10/25/retail-workers-confess-using-the-hard-sell-to-pitch-credit-cards/
2. http://www.nielsen.com/us/en/newswire/2011/in-u-s-men-are-shopping-more-than-ever-while-women-are-watching-more-tv.html
3. http://www.npr.org/templates/story/story.php?storyId=98184836

Chapter 6

1. http://www.cnbc.com/id/47677957
2. http://smallbusiness.yahoo.com/advisor/5-traits-of-bad-bosses-192202212.html
3. http://deliveringhappinessatwork.com/bad-bosses-can-damage-health-and-happiness/

Chapter 7

1. The Atlantic Monthly, *Broken Windows*, James Q. Wilson and George L. Kelling, March 1982 http://www.codinghorror.com/blog/files/Atlantic%20Monthly%20-%20Broken%20Windows.htm
2. http://www.dailymail.co.uk/debate/article-2025793/Bill-Bratton-American-super-cop-called-Cameron-reveals-halt-hoodlums.html

3. ABC News, *Angry JetBlue Flight Attendant Flees Plane at JRK Airport via Emergency Slide*, August 2010 http://abcnews.go.com/US/jetblue-flight-attendant-steven-slater-arrested-flight-jfk/story?id=11361298#

Chapter 8

1. http://www.howstuffworks.com/personal-finance/budgeting/5-retail-markups.htm#page=4

Chapter 9

1. Tony T. Tran, Dr. Anthony D. Hitchins , *Microbial survey of shared-use cosmetic test kits available to the public*, Journal of Industrial Microbiology November 1994, Volume 13, Issue 6, pp 389-391
2. http://www.prevention.com/beauty/beauty/bacteria-makeup-testers

Chapter 10

1. http://www.time.com/time/business/article/0,8599,1855555,00.html

Chapter 13

1. AOL News, *Wal-Mart Security Employees Fired for Disarming Store Gunman*, 2011 http://www.aolnews.com/2011/02/15/wal-mart-security-employees-fired-for-disarming-store-gunman/.

Conclusion

1. About.com, *Retail Industry Information: Overview of Facts, Research, Data, & Trivia*, 2011 http://retailindustry.about.com/od/statisticsresearch/p/retailindustry.htm
2. CNNMoney, *Fortune 500 2012L: Annual Ranking of America's Largest Corporations*, 2012. http://money.cnn.com/magazines/fortune/fortune500/2012/full_list/

Made in the USA
Middletown, DE
12 December 2016